To Flo,
Praise God for
you! In him,
Paula

The 9th Floor

The 9th Floor

by Paula Kilpatrick

with Cliff Dudley

New Leaf Press
Box 1045, Harrison, Ark. 72601

First printing, April, 1981
Revised Edition, February, 1983

Library of Congress Catalog Card Number: 81-80942
International Standard Book Number: 0-89221-085-0

Dedication

To mother, who suffered through many of my trials and now serves the Lord with a strength and wisdom born in adversity.

Contents

Foreword

WHO, FOR HEAVEN'S SAKE, IS PAULA?

One Wednesday night at church, I heard a phone ringing somewhere. Since there was usually someone near the office, I didn't leave the platform to answer it. My dad was preaching to the faithful midweek minority, and I was interested in catching his gems of wisdom.

But the caller didn't give up easily, and nobody was answering.

R-I-N-G!! "Maybe they'll get it in the nursery," I thought.

R-I-N-G!! "Probably just somebody wanting to ask when church will be over so they'll know what time to pick up their grandmother."

R-I-N-G!! "Well, I wish they would give up and call back tomorrow during office hours!"

R-I-N-G!! "Guess I'd better go." *GO?!* Something inside me underlined that word. I ran. "Hello — May I help you?"

The voice on the other end was not that of just a curious caller. She was way past that stage. Neither was it the voice of a relative of someone at church. She didn't know a soul there. She didn't even know where she was calling. Nor was it someone who should hang up and call back tomorrow. She was planning to be dead by morning. At least that's what she told me.

"And don't try to stop me," she wailed. "I don't have anything to live for. My husband doesn't love me anymore. My children are tired of me. I've been sick so long the doctors hate to see me coming. WHERE AM I? . . . You don't think I'd give you my name and address, do you? So you can call the police to rush out here? You think I'm some kind of a dummy, don't you? You think I'm a . . . a . . . oh, I don't know . . . I don't know anything . . ."

The distraught woman would talk awhile and sob awhile, with speech so slurred I couldn't understand some of her words. But one thing was clear, whatever her problems were, they had pushed her to the point of desperation. For over half an hour I listened and talked back, hoping some word might penetrate the blackness swirling around this poor darling. But the signs weren't good. Our conversation was becoming pointless.

Through the speaker on the wall I could tell that Daddy Jack was finishing and I needed to get back. I turned up the volume.

"Now, Lord," his kind voice came through, "we just pray for some lost soul out there stumbling on the dark mountains of sin, trying to find his way. Satan has blinded his eyes so he can't see how much You loved him and died to pay his ransom. But we know Your arm is not shortened that it cannot save, nor Your ear heavy that it cannot hear. You said You are the Good Shepherd who would leave the ninety and nine who are safe in the fold and go out in the night for one little lamb that's lost its way . . ."

"What? Who is that man talking? What are you trying to do?" my nameless caller yelled into the phone.

Running out of time, words, and possibly patience, I said, "That's my father, and in a minute I'm going to be telling him about your problems, and then we will pray for you. Jesus knows exactly where you are, what your name is, and what you need. One day soon I want you to come here and let us meet you. Goodnight!"

One Sunday morning a few weeks later, I noticed a nice-looking couple and little girl making their way toward the piano after church.

"Hi. I'm Paula," the petite, prematurely gray, fashionable lady told me, her smiling blue eyes searching my face for some sign of recognition.

Paula . . . Who, for heaven's sake, is Paula? I pondered, stalling for time to do a quick recall.

I soon found out. And as you read on, you will, too. And

you'll understand why putting Paula together was a job only the King could do. Now, unlike Humpty Dumpty who couldn't ever be mended, Paula really has it all together. Paula and Charlie—together. Paula and Jesus—together in a way many could covet. He listens to her and she listens to Him. Sometimes He tells her things about people and situations she has no way of knowing.

This lady hasn't been to Bible school and might mispronounce a word. *Specific* may be "pacific," and *famine* come out "phantom." Yet glowing reports and call-back invitations keep coming from pastors wherever she has been. She has to be one of those daughters mentioned in Joel 2:28!

—Anna Jeanne Price

Preface

I've known almost every heartache a person can know. Loneliness was my constant companion, along with rejection, hurt, despair, loss of loved ones, attempted suicide and incurable diseases.

In the eyes of men there was no hope for me. A traumatic childhood, disease, drugs, alcohol, hypnotism—all of these had contributed to the fall. My beautiful children had come to view me with eyes of contempt. My marriage was falling apart, as were my body and soul.

Family and friends had given up on me.

I had given up on myself.

Only a miracle could save me and lift me out of the pit I was in. Thank God, the age of miracles is NOT over!

—Paula Kilpatrick

Acknowledgement

Anna Jeanne Price had a very special place in my early Christian experience. She also had a very important part in the writing of this book. Her many hours of labor translating my scribbled notes and organizing my thoughts were vital to the final completion of the manuscript. I appreciate her valuable contribution to the book and to my life.

1
Roots

Roots? You had better believe I had roots—roots of bitterness, loneliness, violence, fighting, and hate. Most of my roots have been nothing but a violent nightmare.

My family roots really began in a wild little town in Mississippi called Stewart. The town was small, and the main attraction was the pool hall and general store owned by my grandfather Augustus "Gus" McGarrh. Train robberies and all other sorts of evil doings seemed to be planned there even though it was never proven.

When my father was twelve, he went to grandfather's store to work, as did his three older brothers, Cook, Creer, and Carmen. Dad was about his daily duties when he heard someone scream at his brother, "You're a cheat, Cook. You're a dirty cheater."

"Who are you calling a cheat?" he heard Cook reply. "You take that back, or I'll pound your head into the wall."

In moments the whole place was like a real scene from a western movie. My father ran toward the commotion and saw the gun.

"Don't shoot! Don't shoot!" he yelled.

He was too late. The bullet screamed from the gun. His father grabbed his chest and fell to the floor. Gus had taken up the fight for Cook, not allowing anyone to question one of his boys. Thus, Gus was the one who was shot instead of Cook.

Slowly, Gus took the pool stick and went for the man who had shot him. He almost beat him to death before Gus fell to the floor dead.

My grandfather's murderer was tried but let go because of lack of evidence!!

The McGarrh brothers selected Cary, my dad, to get revenge. At twelve, they felt he was so young the law would not do anything to him.

My father was filled with hate for grandfather's murderer, and he tried to kill him. Consequently, he was sent to a reform school. When he finally got out of reform school, he was nothing but a mean little boy.

When my father was eighteen, he met my mother, who was only fifteen. They were soon married, with neither of them knowing how to love.

My mother's childhood had been as tragic and lonely as my father's had been. She and her brother Thomas were raised by an invalid "fairytale" step-grandmother.

"Miss Lizzie" made life almost unbearable for the two of them, putting so many work demands on them that they were robbed of their childhoods.

Mama was never allowed to wear new and pretty things to school as other girls did, nor was she allowed to have friends or attend any of the extra activities of the school. So, wanting to escape, she married my daddy.

On their honeymoon they were window shopping when mama stopped suddenly, turned to my daddy, and said, "Oh, Cary, look at those beautiful shoes. Someday I would love to have a pair just like them. All my life Miss Lizzie has made me wear terrible shoes."

"Someday soon I'll get you a pair just like them!" he said with a smile.

The very next day daddy went back to the store and bought them. He wanted so very much to give something to the woman he loved. The shoes were very expensive for those times—$3—and daddy didn't have any money, so he wrote a "hot" check. His bride had to have those shoes no matter what the cost. Little did he know what the cost would be.

Somehow the store owner knew the check was no good and called the police.

The police arrived and remarked, "At last we have a McGarrh —and red-handed at that."

The next day, four days after the marriage, daddy was tried, sentenced, and sent to the Mississippi State Prison. The sentence: three years—one for each dollar.

After being there for about six months, dad was released, thanks to his uncle who knew the governor and used his influence.

When daddy realized that power, he made up his mind to always know and heavily support whatever governor was in office. Many times thereafter that decision paid off.

His stay in prison had a pronounced ill effect on their marriage, and never again would the blossoms of romance be theirs.

When he got out of the penitentiary, he was like a Dr. Jekyll and Mr. Hyde. Years later he told us over and over how prison guards would draw a line and dare the men to step over the line and that if they did, they would be shot down.

My father saw many prisoners walk over that line because they simply did not want to live, and that would be their fast escape. Many times daddy would cry over the things that he had seen in the penitentiary.

He was determined to never go behind bars again and that he would always have enough money to pay off anyone.

Daddy made sure we had plenty of everything, even in the '30's when money was hard to come by. He owned a restaurant, but that was a cover for his "bootlegging" under the counter. Try as the sheriff would, he could never catch him. There were secret trap doors all over our house which attached to the restaurant. I can remember daddy swinging through those doors to get the liquor.

I often wondered why everybody else had very little while we always seemed to have plenty to eat, more than enough. Soon I found out it was because of the illegal whiskey.

Daddy was a compulsive gambler. He would bet on most anything—cards, dice, ball games. And he bet big. He must have won—and lost—several fortunes in his lifetime.

Gambling created a very strong feeling of insecurity in the family. I can remember daddy saying jokingly, "Come here, Paula. I'll just throw you in the game." I was never completely convinced that he wasn't serious.

My father loved my mother very much, but when he got drunk, he was a very mean man. He would get his gun and hold it on mama for hours and hours. All of us kids would go to her rescue and try to pull him off of her.

My three sisters and one brother (Margaret, Phyllis, Linda Kay [Lin], and Douglas) and I were brought up in a world of fear.

Because of all that violence, I developed a terrible fear of men. Although I loved my father, I also feared him. It was not until later in life that I learned how to stand up to him.

My life was a totally violent nightmare. No way did I have even the semblance of a normal childhood. I seemed to spend most of my life in closets crying. I didn't want to come out because I didn't want to face people. I constantly lived in fear.

I never knew what to expect when I came home from school. If my father had been drinking, I knew there had been or would be trouble. When he was drunk, I would be scared to go in the house. I knew he had his gun in his pocket, and that terrified me!

Yet, when he wasn't drinking, he was so sweet and kind. He would hold us kids on his lap for hours and hours. In fact, we would have to beg him to let us get down because he always asked, "How much, how much do you love me? Please tell me how much you love me."

Until the day he died, he continued to ask, "How much do you love me?" It was so sad that he never felt loved.

We children never knew how to give our father love either. Our life was lived in such extremes of tension and unrest. My father tried to love us. I can remember when we were small children how we knew not to take daddy with us when we were going to buy shoes because of his fascination for high heels. If he went with us, we would all come back with pairs of high-heeled shoes even though we were very small.

Also, daddy did not want any of us to work. He seemed to put us on a pedestal. As a matter of fact, he didn't even want us to learn.

To me there seemed to be nothing but terror and tension. I'm sure there were times of happiness, but they were few and far between. When daddy drank, it was a nightmare for all of us. He would never hurt us kids but instead would lash out with all of his hate and anger at mama.

When mama could stand it no longer, she would pack up the kids and go to California. Even though I was afraid of daddy, I couldn't leave him, and I would stay with him, thinking that somehow as a ten-year-old I could help and love him. Oh, how very much I loved him.

In the midst of all of this turmoil a new baby brother was born. When he was nearly two years old, he caught a cold, and we thought nothing of it. I went to school as usual, and when I came home that afternoon, he was in the hospital. The next day he died of diptheria!

After the funeral parlor prepared the body, they brought the casket and put it in the living room, as was the custom in those days.

We were troubled because daddy wouldn't quit crying and became horrified when he went over to the casket, picked up the body, and began walking all over the house crying, "Why? Why? Why?"

I thought, "Why doesn't he put him down?" It hurt me so to see my daddy suffer. In all my life I had never seen my father so broken.

My mother and father almost lost their minds over the death of my brother. There wasn't really anything anyone could have done, but they blamed themselves because they thought that he only had the croup. The entire family was quarantined for six weeks; we had to stay in the house during the entire quarantine.

During this time in my life I didn't have anybody I could talk to except my girlfriend Ren. Ren understood me. We'd go off together to a quiet place and cry.

Much of my childhood was so horrible that I blocked years of it out of my mind. I had fears of so many things.

One of my greatest fears was bridges. Whenever we would come to a bridge, I would beg my father to stop and let me walk across to the other side. I would get hysterical.

His answer would always be, "You're not going to walk across; you're going to ride."

He would stop in the middle of the bridge and say, "Now, I'm going to throw you off, Paula Baby."

"Daddy, daddy, please don't. Please don't!" I'd plead, terrified beyond description.

He was just playing with me, but the scars of that fear stayed deep within me for years to come and were another hindrance to reaching out and loving others.

Perhaps we children didn't know how to give and take love because our parents didn't know either. Daddy always wanted to be affectionate toward mother. But mother would just stiffen up when he came close to her. She did love him, however, or she couldn't have stayed with him all those years not ever knowing what he was going to do.

In one of his gambling ventures he lost the restaurant. We moved to a nice farm and stayed there about two or three years. It was a time of peace, or at least more peace than I had known before. I can never remember really having "peace," but I guess I did have some "happiness." I didn't know the difference between happiness and peace then. And happiness had a way of ending rather abruptly in our house.

One time when mother left my father and went to California, he devised a quick plan to get her to return. I had stayed behind as always with daddy.

I was so small for my age that everyone called me Midget, and that name stuck all through high school. One morning daddy came to me and said, "Midget, today I'm going to take you over to the hospital in Winona and get your tonsils taken out. Baby, that will not only make you grow, but it will also bring back mama and the kids."

Before I had time to answer or knew what was happening, I was at the hospital on the operating table, and they were taking out my tonsils. I was terrified, and when I came to, it was worse.

When I opened my eyes, daddy was leaning over me laughing, saying, "Honey, you can get up now. We've got to go home."

We walked a mile in the hot sun with me throwing up blood. He even bought me a hamburger. It's a miracle that I didn't die. When we got home, grandma was horrified and put me to bed. She gave me only broth for the next week.

Moments after we got home, I could hear daddy giving the operator mama's telephone number in California.

"Hello, honey, this is Cary. Something terrible has happened! I had to take little Paula to the hospital for surgery. She had her tonsils removed. You'll be coming right home, won't you?"

I looked up and saw a satisfied grin all over his face. Suddenly it disappeared, and he hung up the phone. I knew then his plan hadn't worked. Mama had said no!

It didn't really upset me. Even at that young age I didn't expect her to come home. I knew that my mother had a tormenting fear of daddy because she never knew when he might use that gun and kill her.

Not long after the phone call, daddy said, "Baby, get your things ready. We are going to California to be with mama." I was so excited.

The next morning daddy, his friend Sam Gardner, and I drove non-stop to San Francisco.

After our quick trip to California to bring mama back, daddy decided California would be a good place for us to live. World War II was in progress, and there were plenty of jobs available in the San Francisco area in the defense plants and shipyards.

Daddy went out first and got his job in the shipyard, and the family followed. Mama was working in a large department store, and my sister Margaret was also working, so we did quite well financially as a family.

I was about twelve years old when we moved to California, and I had matured quite fast for my age. I started smoking out behind the house. I really don't know why I did it; I guess it made me feel like a big shot.

Even at an early age I wondered why mama stayed with daddy with all the torture he put us through as a family. It didn't seem to be once in a while either. It seemed to be a continuous thing, and I felt sorry for my oldest sister because most of the responsibilities of the family fell upon her to take care of us and do a lot of the cooking.

Violence continued to plague our family. One day mama told me that all the love she had for daddy was gone. She related that he had been choking her almost to death in one of his drunken rages. And she continued that if the doorbell had not rung, she really believed he would have killed her then and there.

It seemed we hadn't been in California very long when my mother told daddy that she was expecting a baby and wanted to return to Mississippi to give birth and then return to California. This really seemed to give my mother hope and helped her get over the grief of losing our little brother Ronnie.

As quickly as we had moved to California, we quickly moved back. One day daddy just came in and said, "We're moving to Cleveland, Mississippi."

One of the biggest shocks of my life occurred when I saw the "house" in which we were going to live. It was a shack! It was a house built for the migrant workers who worked on the farms. It was not painted, and the floors had cracks in them. There was no electricity or plumbing, and daddy said we'd live there while he built us a new house.

I was so embarrassed, and, of course, I didn't want anybody to know where we lived. When I would go out on a date, I would have them drop me off miles from the house.

In the midst of all this I became more and more withdrawn. I hid the fear, unhappiness, frustration, and anguish of living in that shack while we waited to move to a better house.

Here I am at age six.

As teenagers my friend, Patsy Miller, and I "pose" for a candid picture.

My parents' style of dress during their younger days reflects the fact that they wanted good things in life.

2
Man on a String

Within I was filled with insecurity, fear, and turmoil; outwardly I appeared more normal. I started dating a boy by the name of George Fletcher. I went "steady" with him, but to me that meant very little.

One day he came over with his twenty-one-year-old roommate, Charles Kilpatrick. I was not quite sixteen and was very excited because I thought he was the most gorgeous man I had ever laid eyes on. He had thick black hair and green eyes.

I didn't even mind that he came to the shack except that when he came over, I happened to have my hair put up in socks and an old sundress on that I had made in home economics class. I wasn't much of a seamstress, and that dress proved it!

I wanted to date Charlie more than anything in the world.

Also, it was a real challenge to me because he didn't even give me a second look. So I simply said to George, "George, I want to date Charlie."

He said, "Paula, you've got to be kidding. You're going steady with me."

I replied, "George, if you don't get me a date with him, I won't date you anymore."

Finally he condescended and said, "O.K., Paula, O.K."

He went to Charlie and told him that I would like to have a date with him.

Charlie said, "George, you must be kidding. *You* can date her, but *I'm* not going to date that ugly girl."

George persuaded Charlie by saying, "If you don't date her, she won't date me anymore."

Finally, Charlie gave me a call.

When he came to pick me up, I had spent all day getting myself pretty. At that moment, he told me later, he fell in love with me.

We went to the VFW dance despite the fact Charlie hardly knew how to dance. He tried the best he could, but all he did was walk all over my feet. Right then and there I decided that I didn't like him, and I left him the whole night and danced with anyone who would ask me.

We finally left the dance and had hardly gotten in the car when he pulled me to him and kissed me. That was the first time anyone had kissed me on my first date. I was in total shock. I went in and told my mother, "Do you believe that thing, Charlie, grabbed and kissed me on my first date!" I quickly decided I didn't want to ever see or date him again.

But he kept coming to see me. Even though he said I looked just like Elizabeth Taylor, I didn't like him. I couldn't run him off after that, even though I could never say I loved him. Little did I know then it would be years before I would ever learn how to love.

Charlie and George didn't have to come to the shack for long to see me. Daddy had finished a beautiful home just outside of Cleveland. Once again our lives seemed to settle somewhat. Mama was very active in the Christian Church, and daddy actually became a deacon. The whole family was attending church quite regularly.

Mama loved to entertain and was always inviting the preacher and his wife out for dinner, or the special speakers that we'd have from time to time. However, an unseen tension continued in our household because we never knew if daddy was going to stay sober the afternoon or not. Daddy seemed to have his booze hidden everywhere. At times we thought it was funny, but then it wasn't funny any longer because of his extreme anger.

Daddy's most prized possession was his father's gun. Whenever he drank, he had to get the gun down and begin terrorizing mama with it. Tension and terror permeated our house and each of us children.

In school, however, I tried to cover the fact that my home life was miserable. By the time I was in tenth grade I acted a little like a clown—trying to put on a happy face to cover the torment that was inside. I laughed and laughed and pretended to be happy. My friends thought I was very funny, but inside was emptiness, hate, hurt, and loneliness.

I really didn't understand myself, and I wasn't going to let anybody get close enough to ever find out who I was.

I had actually started dating when I was fourteen. One man I dated was twenty-five and a drinking friend of my father's. His name was Curtis, and he treated me like a queen. He didn't make any demands of me, and all he ever did sexually was just peck me on the cheek.

It wasn't long before I learned to twist guys around my finger. Yet, all the time I was frightened to death of men and certainly didn't want to have any close relationship with any.

One time I was actually going steady with three or four guys at the same time, and supposedly I fooled every one of them. Once I got their interest, I didn't like them anymore.

For some reason I was very popular, and I ran around mostly with the rich. Daddy had bought a big old beautiful Buick convertible, and I was so proud of that car. Riding in it made me feel like

I was really somebody. Daddy also had a Model A Ford coupe, and he loved that car just about as much as he loved anything.

He couldn't stand my vanity, and at least once a week he'd come driving up in that old Model A to pick me up from school. I wanted to have him come to get me, but, of course, I always wanted him to come in the convertible.

It seemed that to spite me he would come in the old Model A Ford. I was so ashamed of it. To me it represented us being poor, and I knew that if anybody saw me ride in that car, they would laugh.

He'd pull up along side of me, and I'd pretend that I didn't even know who it was. He wouldn't let me get by with that. He'd honk the horn and yell out the window, "Come on. Get in. Get in the car, baby, and I'll take you home."

I'd say, "Go on, dad. I'm not riding in that."

He'd laugh and laugh and follow me all the way if I walked. "Come on, baby," and he'd just laugh.

I'd say, "Daddy, go on. Get out of here. I don't want to ride in that. Go on." Finally, like some strange game we were playing, I'd get in, but I'd hide on the floor until we got home. Daddy seemed to thrive on tormenting me and everybody else in the family.

One time my mother was in the barn milking the cow when we lived on a farm. Daddy heard her in the barn milking, so he quietly shut the door and locked it on the outside and then went about his work. He forgot her, and as a result she was locked in there all day. Well, when he finally remembered it, he sneakingly opened the door and planned to run, but before he got out of the way, she hit him with the milk bucket.

The torment and abnormality of my home life helped turn other parts of my life into a tangled mess. I was dating Charlie and going steady with George, and at the same time I was engaged to Curtis.

One time Curtis and I went to one of the proms. I noticed Charlie was there with some of his college buddies, and he had been drinking a little.

Normally, Charlie was not a drinker, and that one drink

loosened him up enough that he could talk freely to me. I danced Curtis down to where Charlie was, and Charlie completely ignored me. All of a sudden something within me saw that challenge again, and I wanted Charlie back.

The very next day I called him and told him I had something I wanted to tell him. Of course that was a lie; I had nothing to tell him and was just trying to think up some excuse to get him back.

As soon as I got him back, I didn't like him again. In the midst of all this, Charlie had fallen deeply in love with me.

My life was like an afternoon TV soap opera, but it was my life and it wasn't funny. It was complex, fearful, and frightening to the extent that almost every day I contemplated an easy way to commit suicide just trying to end it all.

I continued to lead Curtis on while at the same time trying to devise a way of getting out of a possible marriage.

One day daddy took me for a ride in the field in the truck and said, "Baby, you cannot marry Curtis. The engagement is off. The wedding is off."

I protested, "But, daddy, we're going to get married in June."

He said, "No, baby, you're not marrying him in June. I don't want you to marry anybody like me. He gambles and he drinks, and he'll do nothing but get you pregnant and run off in a drunk. You're not going to marry him, and that's that. No wedding. It's off."

Deep within I smiled and thought, "Thank you, daddy, for getting me out of that." Then I looked at him, and I said, "Well, *you're* going to have to tell Curtis it's off."

Daddy wasn't scared of anybody. He went to Curtis and said, "It's off. You're not marrying Paula."

It wasn't long until Curtis came over and moped around. I really didn't mind, but I was glad to be out of the whole mess.

About a week or so later all of my conniving and scheming finally caught up with me. I went on a date to the VFW Club with one of my steadies. That night George and Charlie also decided to go to the dance to see what was going on. When they walked in, I was caught. All three of the men that I was going steady with were there. So Charlie and George decided to just leave, and I was stuck with Joe.

On their way home Charlie and George decided they would fix me. They pulled their car off the road into a ditch to pretend that there had been an accident.

When Joe and I left the dance, we passed the car. It was lying in the ravine, and I said, "Look, Joe, Charlie's car has had a wreck."

We stopped and got out of the car. I went running toward Charlie. He looked as though he was in the car dead. I was screaming and hollering, "Charlie! Charlie!" Finally I pulled the door open.

As I got down near him to see if he was breathing or not, he got a strange grin on his face. He looked up at me and said, "Paula, will you marry me?"

In front of George and Joe and all the others who had gathered around I said, "Yes, yes, yes, Charlie, I'll marry you."

I guess I could say that because I had no great fear of him, but the next morning when I woke up and was rational, I called Charlie and said, "Charlie, you've got to forget what I said last night. I'm not marrying you or anybody else."

My mixed-up relationship with men stemmed partially from childhood memories. The fighting, shootings, and the cursing that went on in the small restaurant in Stewart seemed to flaunt themselves more and more before me. I would hide under the counter among the ketchup bottles, and the men would sit around the counter, trying to bribe me to talk. As soon as they would turn their heads, I would run away.

Now here I was with a man who had proposed to me, and I was only sixteen. Charlie was kind and bashful. And, oh, how I longed to belong to somebody.

Deep down I wanted to belong to Charlie because he was sweet to me and perhaps he could help me overcome my fear of men. After all, I reasoned, my daddy had just forbidden me marrying Curtis, so perhaps I was being too hasty in turning Charlie down. But my pride wouldn't let me say anything to him.

On my next date with Charlie, we drove to Parchman where my sister Margaret lived. As we were driving along, Charlie suddenly pulled off into a little picnic area and took a ring box out and simply put a ring on my finger. There was no romance, no sweet little words. I suppose he thought that everything had already been said and done in the fake auto accident, and now he was going to hold me to it.

I thought to myself, "The least he can do is to ask me to marry him." But I let him put the ring on my finger.

Then he said, "Now we're engaged."

My quick reply was, "O.K."

When I got home, I was rather excited and woke up my sister and said, "Guess what? Charlie has put a ring on my finger, and we're going to be married."

Her response was, "Well, Paula, you could have done worse. You're getting a good guy. He doesn't talk much but he's O.K."

I went to my dad and showed him, and he was like a mad man at the thought of somebody taking his baby girl away from him, even though one of my other sisters had already been married. There I was with a ring on my finger, and my daddy wouldn't even look at it.

Within three months I had met, been engaged to, and married Charlie.

3
Marriage

I didn't really know anything about men. I thought marriage would be nothing more than eating out every night, going to the movies, dancing, having fun, and getting away from all the bad fights.

I suppose another reason that I wanted to marry Charlie was to get away from Curtis. I had to do something, and Charlie was the only man with whom I thought I could be safe, and he wouldn't put demands on me.

Charlie didn't drink. He didn't smoke. He didn't even cuss.

Charlie loved God, and, for the life of me, I couldn't understand why. Sure, mama had taken us to Sunday school when I was little, and we were active in the Christian Church even at the time I met Charlie. We loved our pastor and ate a lot of fried chicken with him, but I had never found a life-changing experience in Christianity.

When it actually came time for the marriage, I was so frightened that I locked myself in the bathroom and cried my eyes out. I simply could not get myself together. Before long daddy was out in the car getting ready to leave. He said, "If you're not ready, I'm going without you."

So I ran out to the car, my wedding dress floating behind me, screaming, "Daddy, wait for me! Wait for me!"

After the wedding, we took a short honeymoon trip to Biloxi, Mississippi. Our first night was spent in Jackson. I knew nothing about marriage and neither did he; we were both so insecure. The very first night of our honeymoon I got him to sit up and talk with me all night.

All I wanted to do was go home. I cried and cried; I wanted my mama. Finally, towards the wee hours of the morning I put on my negligee, but I had all my undergarments on under it. He did get me to lie down on the bedspread, but that was all. It went on like that for three or four nights before we came together and consummated the marriage. I had that much terror and fear.

Poor Charlie, he married a completely empty shell that was battered and torn and broken like a female Humpty Dumpty. There we were—two kids not knowing how to love. Charlie didn't know how to love. He didn't know how to show it because he hadn't seen it. And there I was also, just a broken mess, not knowing the first thing about love.

Oh, how Charlie tried desperately to get me to say, "I love you," but I couldn't say it. I didn't even know enough about love to speak it.

Charlie was shy and gentle, and before long I was taking advantage of what I considered weakness.

Charlie would have done anything to make me happy, but we both quickly realized that there was no way to make me happy. Humpty Dumpty couldn't be put together again.

When we returned from the honeymoon, we lived with Charlie's mother and father, and they treated me just like their little girl.

I guess Charlie had expected me to get up and cook his breakfast, but I knew nothing about cooking food. My father had brought me breakfast every morning of my life. When I woke up, I woke up mad and gave Charlie another shock in his young married life by cussing him out. Little did Charlie know what he had married.

I had learned to cuss from my father who had given me very systematic teaching. His method of instruction consisted of making a big breakfast and then trying to get me out of bed to eat it. He thought my kicking and screaming when he got me out of bed every morning was funny. I'd scream, "Leave me alone!"

"Then say a cuss word for me."

I'd say a cuss word.

After I'd gotten older, I learned how to stand up to him. The more I would stand up to him the better he liked me because nobody stood up to him. No one ever stood up to Cary McGarrh. No one ever said anything to him unless it was "Yes, sir." Every one of my sisters and brothers referred to him as "Yes, sir." So I learned how to cuss, and he liked that.

He'd tell me to do something, and I'd say something smart and a cuss word at him. One day he threw a can at me for something I said, and it sliced my head open and knocked me to the floor. I got mad and got up cussing.

That moment I decided to run away and went over to my married sister's house and stayed with her for a couple of weeks before I returned home.

When Charlie, my innocent husband, came in to wake me up, I had a flashback, and I let him have it. Charlie backed out of the room and sort of snuck off with that horrified look on his face and ashamedly went to work. That was the last time he ever tried to wake me up in the morning for years to come. He couldn't believe that any woman could ever cuss like I cussed.

When later I told that story to daddy, he thought it was the funniest thing he'd ever heard. When Charlie told him, daddy clapped his hands and was tickled and smartly said, "Yes, Charlie,

I really taught her to lay a man out with words."

That incident had been the first time I'd ever let anybody besides my father hear me cuss. After all, I was a proper lady.

Charlie's mother was so kind and tried to take this "proper lady" under wing. She did everything, and in my clumsy way I'd try to help her.

We lived with Charlie's parents about six months until we found a tiny little house. I mean it was a little, bitty home. It looked something like a doll house.

When we moved into the little doll house, it seemed gorgeous. I was so proud of it that I cleaned it every day. I even washed down the walls. A person couldn't find a crumb any place in that house. As a matter of fact, I kept it so clean that no one could be comfortable in it.

Everyone made fun of me. People would kid me that they would have to bury me with my mop and Babo. It seems I had the habit of following behind visitors, carrying my mop and rag to capture any dirt.

Time passed, and I thought we were having a very normal life—at any rate as far as what I knew was normal. We were attending a little Baptist church at the time. I was even baptized because they wouldn't accept my First Christian Church baptism. I thought that was rather strange, yet I wanted to fit in and didn't protest.

Every day I would see Charlie reading his Bible. It seemed he wanted to read it constantly, and that made me furious. While he was reading the Bible, I would read my *True Story* magazines, thinking of the exciting lives the people in the stories were living while I sat at home with a husband who read his Bible.

I'd turn to him and say, "Charlie, don't you know that it's not really for real?" Instead of saying anything he'd just go to the store and get me more of my *True Confessions* or *True Story*. I could read twenty-five a week since I was a speed reader.

I thought Charlie was such a weak man because he'd give in to everything I wanted to do. My father was so strong, and even though he was very mean, everybody admired that strength in him. Anything I wanted Charlie to do for me, he would just do.

And all that Bible reading just made me think he was weak. After all, wasn't the Bible for the sick-minded, the mentally weak, and those who were just so poor they had nothing else to turn to but God?

I could twist Charlie around my finger anytime I wanted to, and I really didn't like that. I'd make Charlie take me dancing on Saturday nights. It was kind of a deal we had. "You go dancing with me, and I'll go to church with you," I said. And he agreed. He hated it, but he went with me. And I hated it, but I went with him.

Church was so strange. It never seemed to fulfill me. Every time I heard the song, "Just As I Am," (and they played it a lot in that church) I'd run down to the altar. But it seemed that there was nothing there for me.

We sat in church, and all I heard were dos and don'ts. And I was always doing what they said "don't." I felt like a hypocrite all the time because I'd been doing all the things they told me not to do. As a result, our church attendance waned as time passed.

Curtis would still call all the time, and whenever Charlie and I would go dancing, Curtis would be there. This was tormenting Charlie.

Within me I was constantly wondering if I had made a mistake by marrying Charlie. With Charlie there was never any excitement. He was just too "good" as far as I was concerned to give me any fulfillment in my life.

But I was determined that we were going to have a happy, normal life. I told Charlie we just had to have a baby. So our first child—a precious little boy—was born after we were married two years.

I threw everything I had into that child. I was a possessive mother beyond that which was normal. I had a constant fear that something was going to happen to our little Tommy. As a result, Charlie and I both wrapped our lives around our child. This was the first thing that I'd ever had in life that I felt really belonged to me.

I had the gnawing feeling that something was going to take

Tommy away from me. I felt this so strongly that it became an obsession with me. For hours I would stand by his bed to make sure he wouldn't choke. If he coughed, I ran; and I would become almost hysterical if his eyes even twitched. I could hardly let him out of my sight.

Charlie also was close, but he seemed to be able to handle things easier than I. If Tommy had a speck of dirt on him, I'd wipe it off. I couldn't stand for it to be there a second.

Despite my overprotectiveness and oddities, our lives were calm during the two years after Tommy was born. We had drifted further and further from the church. We were not really evil, but we certainly weren't "saints." Charlie simply worked. I kept house, and our lives became a daily routine.

We didn't worry a lot about money because we didn't have much. We were just crazy enough that we'd use our last dollar to go to a movie or go to the dance. In the back of our minds, we knew Charlie's parents would bail us out if we really got in financial trouble.

During this two year period we spent a lot of time visiting both of our parents. One night in the wee hours of the morning there was a bang on the door. It was mama and daddy's neighbor looking for them because their house was on fire. Their beautiful home was burned to the ground. They had spent the night with Margaret in Greenville, about ten miles away. Many in town thought the fire was suspicious. Some even thought that my father had set it for the insurance.

Of course, Charlie and I scrambled out of bed and immediately went to the scene of the fire where we saw my father standing, sobbing uncontrollably. He was holding the charred remains of his father's gun.

I turned to Charlie and said, "Charlie, look, he's holding the gun. Thank God it's burned. Thank God it's burned. Perhaps now he'll realize that he can never hold it to mama's head again." They had lost everything!

Charlie helps me cut our wedding cake. I didn't know what marriage was all about.

4
Hypnotized

It wasn't long until daddy was rebuilding another home in Stewart, back where the whole mess seemed to have started. The violence, the jealousy grew worse and worse.

One night the final fight occurred. Daddy had mama down on the floor in the kitchen choking her. She found the handle of a cast iron skillet and hit him on the head with it as hard as she could. It was the first time mama had ever struck back. It not only stunned daddy in his senses, but it stunned his ego. He came crying to us and wept and wept, "She hit me over the head. I can't believe that she would do that to me." In his pride and arrogance he said, "I'm going to file for a divorce." He did. That skillet could have cracked his skull, but all it really hurt was his pride.

Mama took Phyllis and Lin and moved to Chicago. This was

the final separation. The effect on us children was very traumatic. Mama and Phyllis found work there and started life over, if it's ever possible to do that. It wasn't long until they called, wanting me to come and visit them. They felt I needed some relief from the boredom and complaints of housekeeping. They sent me the money for a train ticket—not only once but several times. It seems I made that trip a thousand times.

The next two years were the beginning of a constant downhill run for Charlie and me. He was just a bystander watching me rush in my race to destruction.

The first trip to Chicago was very exciting. We all decided to go to the Aragon Ballroom and see what was going on. We got a table and were just going to sit there and watch. None of us had really been to any place that was this exciting.

By now I was used to drinking, and I should say quite heavily. We were kidding which one of the men we were going to pick up. My sister stuck out her foot and tripped a guy as he went by our table. He didn't fall down all the way, but he didn't appreciate it. He was a tough-looking dude. He turned to us and said, "How dare you?" It almost scared me witless. I thought to myself, *He's going to bash us in the head.*

It wasn't long before there were several guys sitting around us. After all, we didn't realize it was a place where guys came to pick up girls. They were telling us how they came in to dance, and all I could say was, "Well, I'm not going to dance with you." I looked at this guy and said, "You'd have to get my mother's permission before I'd ever dance with you."

He asked mother and, of course, she said, "Yes." I still wouldn't dance with him.

On my trips to Chicago I always took Tommy with me. Every time I got on that train to leave for Chicago it was almost death for Charlie. He never knew if I was coming back. Our marriage was hanging by such a thin thread that I'm sure he thought I was going to cut it loose at any moment.

I picked up the Chicago paper and saw an advertisement of a hypnotist appearing for six weeks at this plush ballroom. I begged the family to take me. I'd never seen anything like that. Finally after pleading and begging and carrying on, they agreed to take me.

We got there and the place was packed. You could just tell all the women were chasing after this man. I couldn't get over it. Then I saw him—wow! He was the handsomest man I'd ever laid eyes on—white hair, green eyes. To this point I had never had any problems with sexual lust thoughts. I was really a rather frigid person, but there was something about this man that excited me with an excitement that I'd never felt before. I had on a beautiful white lace dress. It was full. At that time I had very long black hair. If I had known at that very moment how this man would become a destructive tool of Satan in my life, I would have gotten up and run, for the experience that was about to happen would be responsible for many of the trials and troubles and agonies that I would experience in later life.

Suddenly I was shocked because he looked directly at me with his cold eyes staring into mine and said, "Young lady, would you come up here please?"

My immediate response was, "No," but I said, "I won't come up unless you get my mother's permission."

He turned to my mother and asked, "May your daughter come up?"

"As long as you don't harm her," she replied.

Haltingly I walked forward to the stage.

Behind me I could hear the screams of the other women. "Take me! Take me!" There probably were fifteen or twenty who were jumping up and down wanting to be up there with this gorgeous man. He politely told them all to sit down, then asked if I would sit in a chair. Smiling and ever so gently looking into my eyes, he said, "This girl looks like she'll be a good subject."

Then to me directly he said, "Young lady, look into my eyes." He started counting, "One, two, three." I could barely hear "four" and I was gone. What you read will be what was told me by my mother and sisters.

The man said, "I want you to clap for us."

I did. All the time I looked like I was wide awake, rational, and under absolute control of all my faculties. I wasn't out from under the trance, but it certainly looked like I was not in it. He turned to the audience and said, "When I say a certain word, she's going to look out on the audience, and she's going to see everybody nude." When he said that word, I opened my eyes and I saw everybody nude.

I screamed, "Mother, go get your clothes on! Mother, I can't believe you would do such a thing. Margaret, what are you doing? You should be ashamed of yourself." Everybody was howling with laughter.

"I'm going to put you under a posthypnotic suggestion," he said, "and when you wake up, you'll be down in the audience, but when I say one word, you are going to rush up and give me the most luscious kiss you've ever given anybody."

Mother said everybody laughed, but she was becoming frightened. Before he put me back in the audience, he told them when I came out of the trance I would get up at the sound of the orchestra and would do a most exotic, sexy dance. The way I danced you would have thought I had had lessons all my life. The people stood and applauded and applauded because they had never seen anything like it. A photographer took a photo of me, enlarged it, and put it in his shop window.

In the natural I'm a very clumsy, klutzy person. Anybody who knows me would agree. But something strange laid hold on me, and I went into the real bumps and grinds gyrations.

Everyone was astonished when he put my head on one chair and my feet on another with nothing in between. At the time I probably weighed 105 pounds. He told the audience, "I'm going to stand on her stomach. It won't hurt her." With nothing supporting me, he stood on me and I didn't bend. He even jumped up and down, and I wouldn't bend. He must have weighed at least 180 pounds.

He told me to return to my seat, and now I was awake. I could hear everybody laughing. I asked, "Mother, what went on?" Suddenly I heard him say this word. I calmly got up from my seat, went up on the stage, and kissed him like I'd never kissed anyone before. It sent my head spinning.

After he'd finished his act, he came and asked me to come and sit in a booth with him. I was not in a trance then. I was fully aware of what was going on. He said to me, "Paula, you cannot leave until I give you this certain word."

He'd already given me these instructions under the trance so I indeed became a slave to him. He said, "If you leave before I tell you to, you are going to feel like you are stuck to the chair. If you try to get up, you won't be able to move. It will be like you are stuck to gum."

When mama and the girls wanted to go, for some reason I didn't want to go. I didn't know why, but I just could not leave. Then the hypnotist came over to me, and I felt relieved. I turned to mama and the girls and said, "Come on, let's go. What are you waiting for?"

He said to me, "Now you come back tomorrow night. In fact, you are coming tomorrow evening at eight o'clock." And I did.

As soon as we got home, mother could sense I was restless. In the morning when I woke up, I was restless.

"Well, Paula, what's wrong with you?" asked mother.

I said, "Oh mama, I just want to go and see him again. I just can't wait to see him again."

That night I saw how he had manipulated me as he discovered another good subject.

For that trip I stayed in Chicago for six weeks and returned home. Now that I had experienced THAT man, that awesomeness, that look, Charlie now seemed further in distance than I ever thought possible. He knew something in me was different. I began changing into another personality. Before this he had told me I was sweet. Now I was coarse, bitter, and mean. It seemed I went out of my way to make his life miserable. My trips to Chicago and the effects of the hypnotism erased any desire I'd ever had to make my marriage work. I didn't care, and it about wiped Charlie out.

It wasn't long until I returned to Chicago, and, of course, the hypnotist was back. This time I was there for two or three weeks. He asked me out to lunch.

"Well, I might go with you," I said.

"Come on, Paula, we'll just go for lunch."

I didn't tell mother anything. I just told her that I was going out for lunch and that I was going to the Loop.

She said, "Paula, you can't go to the Loop. You can't get there by yourself." It made me so mad because everybody always treated me that way. Daddy treated me like that. I was that dumb thing that could do nothing. Charlie had treated me that way, and now here was mother telling me the same. But I was going to fool them all. I simply got in a cab and told them where to take me. I remember feeling so brave and strong when I commanded, "Driver, take me to the Palmer House."

After what seemed a very long ride—and a very expensive one at that—I went to the designated restaurant and said to the head waiter, "I'm here to meet Mr. John Doe."

The waiter, with a smile, said, "Ma'am, he's waiting for you."

When I got to the table, I said, "Now, John, don't you hypnotize me."

"Paula, you know that nobody would do under hypnotism what they wouldn't do naturally." Even that scared me because I didn't know what I would or would not do.

"Paula," he continued, "I can't believe anybody could be as naive as you."

"What do you mean?"

"You intrigue me all the more because of either your brilliance or your dumbness, but either way it's exciting."

Even at that I didn't know what he was talking about. I was just a country bumpkin, I guess. Then he shocked me with, "Paula, I can't believe you. Haven't you been to bed with anybody before? Haven't you had a fling, an extra-marital thrill?"

"For heaven sakes, John, no!"

"Well, Paula, don't worry; anything that's against your morals you wouldn't do." Then smiling, he said, "Why don't we go to my room and just talk and talk."

"Well, I *would* like to have a picture of you," I commented.

"They're all in my room, and if you want one, that's where you'll have to get it."

I wanted a picture of him so bad. He'd promised time and time again to bring one to me but always said he'd forgotten it. Then I wondered, *Forgot—my eye! I bet it was all part of his master plan.*

"John, couldn't I just stay here in the lobby and you bring it to me?"

"Oh, I suppose. But, Paula, come on up. It won't matter."

"John, you promise?"

"I promise. I promise I'll not do anything you don't want me to do."

When we got to the room, the first thing he did was grab and kiss me. I let him do it. I'll have to admit the stars and the sirens went off with that kiss. Then he pushed me down on the bed. I became frightened and started crying.

"I can't believe it. Paula, I can't believe it," he said. At that he let me up. He just stood there shaking his head saying, "I just can't believe it." Obviously this man and his looks were used to conquering dumb little girls like me.

When I walked out of his room, I really thought that was the last time I would see him, but it wasn't. The next day he called me. I told him I was going back to Baton Rouge.

"Paula," he said, "you call me a month from now," and he gave me the day and time. Believe it or not, I did just that and had no control of whether I should or should not do it.

When I got home, I was so depressed. Never had I been in such a state of depression. I hardly knew what to do to handle it. I hardly noticed Charlie—period.

I know now that he wouldn't have wanted to live without his son, and he certainly couldn't bear the thought of anyone else raising the boy. I know now that hypnotism is one of the worst devices Satan could create. Every time I hear of someone glibly going to a hypnotist, I want to scream and yell, "Stop, you don't know what you are fooling with!" Somehow God finally delivered me from the demonic influence of that evil man, but the scares would not be delivered as easily.

Supernatural things now had a great attraction for me. Instead of the hypnotist routine, I began going to fortune tellers. I found a beautiful lady who told me that she was of God, an ordained preacher.

The first time I went to her, she had me sit in a very dimly-lit room. She looked as though she was praying, and when she opened her eyes, she began telling me where my husband worked, my father's name, about adventures, and about my experience with the hypnotist. She said these things were putting the depression in my life. She told about my father having a rare disease and that I also was going to get it.

I was so impressed with her that I took her to mama and my sisters. I thought that was the greatest thing I'd ever heard of. I would read my horoscope every day to see what I should or shouldn't do. I had no idea what my dabbling with hypnosis and fortune tellers would cost me in the days ahead.

I never did tell Charlie about the hypnotist, but he knew that I was different and that I'd pretty much lost all interest in many things.

5

The Snake Pit

When Tommy was almost three, I was pregnant again. Our little baby boy was born two months prematurely and died when he was two days old. Charlie and I both felt such a terrific sense of loss, and for a few short weeks it brought us closer together. Two years after that our Karen was born. When I held that little baby in my arms, I thought, "This is it; this is what happiness is all about." Oh, how wonderful it is to just hold, rock, and care for babies. They don't reject you. They don't push you away. How I loved these little ones.

At that time my sister, Lin, who was about fourteen, was ready for high school. It was evident that Chicago was no place for her to be living—that little country girl from Mississippi. She was so lonely she began to associate with some kids who weren't very nice. She was with a bunch of little gangsters who were joy riding, which means stealing a car for the thrill of the ride and then returning it. I talked Lin into coming to Baton Rouge where we lived, to visit us for the summer. That visit lasted for four years.

It was so much fun having Lin with us. We were so much alike in our actions. People even thought we looked alike. Lin was such a gorgeous creature. Even the male teachers wanted to date her. I couldn't wait for her to come home from school. I'd have coffee ready, and we'd sit down and talk about her boyfriends. It was such a happy time for us. Sometimes she would come piling in the bedroom with Charlie and me. We both loved her so very much. We were a real close family.

At the time, Charlie and I did some drinking with the man and his wife who lived next door. Charlie just endured it. He always said it seemed all his friends were no more than an overflow of my friends.

During that time Charlie had gotten a job as an auditor for Firestone. While he was out travelling, Lin and I had a great time. There were no demands. We ate when we wanted to, got up when we wanted to. We didn't do anything seriously wrong, except spend all the money Charlie sent home. It wasn't long until Charlie had to quit his job and come home because we'd spent all the money and we'd forgotten to pay the bills. Also, he just couldn't stand to be away from the children. I was so dumb. I thought he was just sending us the money and we could have fun on it. It never occurred to me that I had to pay bills with it, and never dreamed he was sending it to put it in the bank.

I was amazed at Lin when Charlie did come home, for she looked at him and asked, "Why did you quit your job? We were so used to our own ways. Now you're going to spoil all of that." He couldn't believe that those words came out of Lin!

Charlie went to work for a food chain as manager and was there four or five years. Life was just so monotonous. Deep down in my heart I was grieving because of the breakup of mama and daddy. They were divorced after twenty-seven years of marriage. Daddy was alone, and I worried about him day and night. Yes, I was afraid of him at times, but my desire to be loved was stronger than that fear. I would lie awake many nights just thinking of him, if he was all right or if he was hurting or lonely, whatever. For some reason or other I knew that mama could take care of herself, but I knew daddy was helpless.

Soon Charlie and I moved to Shreveport, Louisiana, where he had taken a good job with the state charity hospital.

In the meantime mama had gotten away from God and started drinking—the very thing she couldn't stand about daddy. It just horrified me seeing her that way and the things it was doing to her. She'd just take one drink and get as giggly and silly as could be. Now she was smoking also.

In spite of these varied experiences, I was still a very fearful person about getting into the world. I found a lot of things in my search, but I didn't find love.

After we went to Shreveport, Lin got married, even though I'd advised her not to. I felt so sorry for her because she, like myself, had never felt love either. She married mostly trying to *find* love, but soon after she was married, she discovered her husband didn't want her. It wasn't long until her marriage ended.

We bought a home in Shreveport. The children were in school, and Charlie's job gave us a very adequate income. YES, we should have been happy, but there was a void in our lives which we never allowed God to fill. We seemed to know so little about God. We didn't even know how to ask Him to fill that emptiness in us.

When we moved to Shreveport, Charlie and Tommy started travelling. They were into dog training all over the United States. On occasion I would travel with them. However, I enjoyed being alone. I could then do as I pleased. I often withdrew into my bedroom very, very depressed and full of fear. I just wanted everybody—family, children, and all—to leave me alone, just leave me alone. I no longer cared.

Charlie was wanting to get away from me and all my problems. He and Tommy had thrown themselves into fishing, hunting, and dog training. Tommy was winning many dog trials and trophies. Charlie was very proud of him, in fact, to the point he neglected Karen and me.

When my children were babies, I could really love them. But after they were older, I could hardly love them because I was afraid they wouldn't love me back. As a result, I didn't show them much love. It was so hard for me to bring them to me and kiss them the way I wanted to. I picked up the same spirit from my father, and I would say over and over, "Do you love me, and do you love your daddy? Who do you love most?"

They'd say, "Daddy," and I would want to go throw myself out the window!

Charlie loved me, but he couldn't display his love. He was not the type. It was very hard for him to show his feelings. He, too, felt he was going to be rejected. He always had a battle of being rejected, even more than I because I could holler and get over it where he'd get it locked up inside him. I could say, "I'm leaving you. That's it. I'm leaving," and pack the car, run off for awhile—maybe just go somewhere and have a drink and come back, but he couldn't do that.

I started drinking beer on weekends. I would always wait until five o'clock on Friday because if you do that then you're not an alcoholic. I would not be like my daddy, I thought. I'd always be in control and in charge of my life, but before long I noticed that I was getting meaner when I would drink. I'd do bold things that I normally wouldn't do. For example, if we were out dancing, I'd want to go to the stage, grab the microphone, and sing. I was so lonely I would do almost anything to get attention. I would embarrass Charlie to tears. My singing gave Charlie the nerve to ask other women to dance. He would get a little flirty with the girls when he was drinking.

We could hardly wait for the weekend to come because it was then we would drink. At first it was just a kind of social drink or two. Then it wasn't long until we became weekend drunks. When we'd drink together at home, we would seem to talk a little more, and I was "friendlier" to him. Although he didn't like drinking, he liked that part.

It was about this time that I developed Raynaud's disease, a rare, painful malady which daddy had also suffered. He had had five or six operations for this disease. The doctors cut many of the nerves in his neck. When I told Charlie I had his disease, it made him furious. He screamed, "No, you don't have it. The doctors are crazy. You don't have it!"

This disease affects the nerves and is like frostbite attacking the hands and feet, which become enlarged and turn white. There is no cure and not much relief for it. I was hospitalized several times. It was especially bad in cold weather. There was even a danger of losing fingers and toes, due to gangrene in the advanced stages of the disease. My doctor tried a variation of that surgery, severing a nerve in my neck. This gave me some relief on one side of my body.

I was seeing several doctors who were all giving me different pills—one for this, one for that, pain pills, sleep pills, wake-up pills, diet pills, nerve pills. I was taking fifteen or twenty pills a day, and with my drinking it should have killed me. I know now that God had His hand on me.

On top of everything else, I developed painful, incurable diverticulitis. Severe attacks would send me to the hospital at least once a month. Paying the doctors, the hospital, and drug bills kept us broke. I was becoming a physical and mental wreck.

Going to the hospital soon became routine. Charlie would shove me in the car and take me to the emergency room. I had had too many pills and too much to drink. I couldn't breathe. I'd either be sick or had overdosed, but I'd be lying on the emergency table at least once a month being pumped out. Charlie became so embarrassed that he got to the place he didn't want to take me, and inside he was probably wishing that I would die.

I'd heard that you couldn't smell vodka. I decided that I'd drink it so no one could smell booze on my breath. I drank privately and tried not to let my children know that I was drinking. Charlie would come home and be so angry because I was always making such a fool of myself.

During the week, from early morning until late afternoon, I watched the soap operas. I would dream of their exciting lives, thinking mine was so dull. How I wanted to have that kind of life! But I knew deep within I couldn't. Something in me was keeping me from it.

I had a cute body and I knew it. I didn't want to become involved with anybody. I just wanted to be an enticer of men. I really must have been a tease because no matter who I went to it seemed eventually they all made a pass at me, doctors and ministers alike.

Several pastors came to call on me. I would make sure I had on my shorts or the sexiest clothes I could find when they came. They would make the pass, and, of course, I wouldn't let them, but I enjoyed the flirting. This was because I hated men, and I wanted to get even.

Nothing now seemed to help. The counselling, flirting, or whatever all seemed to fail. I was totally convinced I was a total waste to the human race. I decided that if nature couldn't kill me, I would take matters of death into my own hands, for I no longer willed to live.

I'll wait until Charlie is gone, and then I'll take a bottle of pills and quietly fall asleep, and I'll never know what happened, I thought. How very strange that I never thought of heaven or hell.

The opportunity came very quickly.

One weekend Charlie was gone with Tommy on a dog show. I went to the bathroom and nervously took down the bottle of pills. Slowly but surely I swallowed one after another until the whole bottle was gone. I lay on the bed to die. Much to my surprise, I woke up in the hospital on the ninth floor. I was locked up in the psychiatric ward. It was horrible. One of my neighbors discovered me on the bed when I had not answered the phone, and she called the police. They brought me to the hospital.

A man was on guard. I tried to bribe him all night and cried and cried. The halls were full of people who seemed to be screaming and walking. Truly I was in a snake pit.

The attendants kept trying to quiet me, and the more they told me to be quiet, the more hysterical I became. My stomach had been pumped, and now the effects of the pills and the booze were leaving my system, and I was faced with stark reality. Then, to my shame, a psychiatrist, whom I knew, came to see me. I said to myself, "Paula, act normal. Don't let them think anything is wrong with you." I tried hard, but it seemed the harder I tried to act normal, the more bizarre I became.

After my brief session with the psychiatrist, I called Nell, a friend of mine, who came to the hospital and took me home.

My search for something became more desperate—the horoscopes, the Ouija board, the pills. I was seeking and searching, seeking and searching, looking for something, but I did not know what. I could not find the key to let me out of this prison in which I was so deeply entrenched. I sank deeper and deeper into depression. I tried to withdraw from everybody and everything. I became sicker and sicker, not only physically but emotionally, and my energy had gone. I was losing weight. I kept myself as far as appearance was concerned, but I couldn't continue to hide; I was losing myself. When the children would come home from school, the first thing they did was to come to see how their mother was. Karen would cry when she saw me. Tommy would look at me in despair and ask, "Mother, are you all right?"

My answer would usually be, "I'm fine, Tommy. I'm fine."

They were both so sweet and compassionate, but I would look into Tommy's eyes, and all I would see was pity. I didn't want his pity; I wanted his love. They felt sorry for me, but they did not know what to do.

One night Tommy came in with a friend and found me sprawled on the bathroom floor—dead drunk and overdosed on pills. He gave me mouth-to-mouth resuscitation, and it worked. As I was coming to, I heard the friend walking out of the bathroom saying, "Tommy, let her die. Why don't you let her die. You'd all be better off."

Tommy screamed out, "Oh, don't say that. Don't say that!"

I knew then that he really loved me. I tried to be a good mother when he was a little boy, and I think even at that moment he looked back and remembered me as I was then. The Lord knows he hadn't seen that good mother for many years.

Tommy was now fortunate because he was at college and only came home on weekends. It was like we were all caught up in a wild nightmare. Karen had become hostile. My diverticulitis had gotten worse. Twice when I was at the hospital, I heard the attendants say, "She'll never make it 'til morning." My poor children . . . my poor children!

One time Karen was so full of anguish she stayed home from school for thirty days, and I wasn't even aware of it. When I found out, I started screaming. I didn't want my children to be rude, disobedient, and disrespectful, and yet I couldn't control myself. One night Karen came home, having had a drink or two. When I saw her like that, I started beating on her, slapping her over and over because I didn't want her to be like me. I'll never forget the sadness that was in her face. Karen's a beautiful girl, but much of that sadness is still there.

I would stay awake all night thinking of different ways to commit suicide—by hanging or poisoning or stepping in front of a truck or driving my car in front of a train. It became more real to me that I should try again—that I could do it.

I went to the bathroom and cut my wrist. I was bleeding when Charlie and Tommy came in and caught me. Oh, how ashamed and embarrassed I was. My son saw the blood gushing from my wrist. Oh, how I wanted to die!

Why can't I die? I thought. I didn't want to be like this, but I couldn't help myself, and I knew deep down there was nobody who could help me now. It seemed Charlie, my children, and everybody had given up on me, and I had given up on myself. But I kept thinking, *How can I kill myself?*

I tried seven times using different methods. I'd wait until the children were gone and no one was around. I would turn on the gas stove, but it seemed somebody would always come in. Sniffing the air, they would say, "What is that I smell?"

I would laugh and say, "Oh, it's just a gas leak somewhere," as I began a fake search for the leak. I was always so ashamed and afraid they were going to guess what I'd been up to. At the time I was caught, I would say to myself, "Oh, I've failed again. I can't even kill myself right." The thought never occurred to me where I would spend eternity if I were successful. Would I go to heaven or would I spend it in torment much worse than my present life?

Little did I know that there were those who DID care for me —such as Margie Tibbets, who worked with Charlie, and the Warren family! Later I learned that my sister-in-law, Marie, and my brother were praying for me.

Charlie was miserable. He never knew what he was going to come home to. On his way home he would usually stop by the liquor store and get a six-pack or two of beer and we'd drink. We'd forget to eat and would usually run out and get the kids hamburgers, or Karen would go to her room and watch TV. If I did cook, I was so out of it that we would just have to throw it out. Besides, we would rather drink.

Karen kept it all within her. She never screamed or yelled at me and never told me she hated me.

Tommy only saw me on weekends. I'd embarrassed him so many times. One time he caught me drunk. I said, "Tommy, you hate me, don't you?"

He looked at me with steel eyes, the tears flooding down his face, and with hate he said, "Yes. Yes, I do."

I looked at him and left the room. He followed me. He had become so independent and already trusted nobody.

Whatever would become of us?

6
My Life's Empty

One day I awakened with a new zeal. I thought, "I've got to get out of this place. Maybe I'll get a job. After all, I'm not an invalid. Perhaps that would help me."

I went to work for a very plush restaurant in Shreveport. All I had to do was to be the hostess and greet people. It was a very good job. Most of the men, after I seated them, would offer me a cocktail or coffee, which made it very easy for me to drink on the job. I didn't drink that much, just enough to keep me happy. I'd go home about two o'clock in the morning and drink for most of the rest of the night.

If I wanted to get off early, like eight or nine o'clock, all I had to do was go into a crying session, and they'd let me off.

It was at that restaurant I met a very special priest. He would come in every day with several other priests. He was a very nice looking, well-built man. He would always order a scotch. Somewhere I'd heard that priests were very good counselors. After the fourth or fifth time he came, I decided I would talk to him, and I asked him for an appointment.

His response was, "Sure, I'll be glad to. What time do you want to meet with me?"

We set the day and the time, and he told me where the church was located. When the day came, I went with anticipation that I would get all the answers that I needed, for Charlie and I were ready to call a halt to our marriage.

When I walked into his office, it seemed very strange. He told me to sit down. I noticed that on his door was a little window shade which he pulled down to block out the outside view. He was a perfect gentleman and offered me a cigarette. I became so nervous I thought I would pass out from fright. During our conversation he never asked one thing about our marriage—not one word was said about Charlie and me. He talked about my dress. How lovely I looked. How beautiful I was. My hair was just right. It was nothing but compliments.

I thought it strange and couldn't understand it when he said he couldn't understand why any man would have a problem with me. I wasn't quite sure what this priest was working up to. But I put it out of my mind and waited for the next appointment.

When I saw him again, he said, "Paula, I think it would be best if I would come to your house and get to meet Charlie. But be sure when I get there to tell me to take off my collar because it will make him feel more comfortable, and he'll feel more free to talk."

Charlie wasn't too happy with me for consulting a priest. And when I told him the priest was to come for dinner the next week, he was furious. The priest came, bringing his fifth of scotch. Charlie and I didn't even drink scotch.

As we sat at the table eating, I felt the priest's knees under the table tapping mine. "I'm in his way," I thought, but I'd feel his knees again. I passed it off as an accident. He was a very handsome, sophisticated, brilliant man. I knew that Charlie wasn't too impressed. I didn't invite him to the house again, but he would call and invite himself. We never did get to talking about our marriage.

Then the priest started coming over every evening. He'd call about two o'clock and say, "I think I'll come over tonight and talk with you and Charlie."

I couldn't say anything but, "That's fine."

Every time he came, I could tell Charlie was more resentful. After all, he was coming over every night, and not once did he ever talk to us about our marital difficulties or that God could perhaps be an answer to our problems. The more he came, the bolder he got. It got to the place where almost every night he would say, "Rather than drinking scotch, I feel like I would like to grab a quick beer. Come on, Paula, let's you and I go. Charlie can stay here and watch the movie." He thought he was very slick and that I was gullible. True, I was very much flattered. I knew this priest had an infatuation for me, and that tickled me.

Charlie would just glare and not say a word, and away we would go. I would continually convince myself that the priest, as all priests, was a very godly man. We would get into the car, and he would go around the corners, and I would fall into him. It was a continued game every time we went for that beer. He never made a real forward advance, but I knew the day would come when he would.

Pretty soon the calls came at two o'clock every afternoon, and he would ask if I had anything on, what I had on, what it was like, what did I look like? I just shrugged it off—a lonely man with a crush. Then it hit me, I must be a horrible woman if this man would want me. After all, he's a man of God!

Even though my nerves were stretched almost beyond limits, I would still dare to drive an automobile either stoned on drugs or boozed up on alcohol. For some strange reason it seemed everybody would dodge me. I hadn't had any wrecks. Then one day I had two.

I'd had a little bit to drink, and whenever you add alcohol to barbituates, you are in trouble. I found myself slamming into the back of a car. I was shaking and so frightened and distraught that the policeman, whom I knew, felt sorry for me and said, "Paula, I'll drive you home."

On our way, even though it was very nervy of me, I asked him if he would stop and get me a six-pack of beer. He stopped the car, went into the liquor store, and came out with a carton of beer and then took me home. I'd never had an accident before, and this was only a minor scrape, but I couldn't seem to get hold of myself.

When I walked into the house, I was so depressed I decided I needed a couple of beers to calm my nerves, and I began drinking. I couldn't stand sitting in the house, so I decided I'd go for a ride. In pulling out across one of the intersections, I had another accident. I cracked my ribs and hurt my leg. As a result, I landed in the hospital.

A series of X-rays showed how bad it was, and the doctors decided I should stay there for observation. The next day the priest came by to see me, and as he stood by my bed, suddenly he leaned over and kissed me on my lips. I tried to tell myself he was just being friendly and did that because he felt sorry for me, but I knew that a friendly kiss wasn't like the one he gave me.

Charlie was so upset with me that he decided that I should go visit my mother in California. For some strange reason I got it in my head that he was sending me to a party. I was so mixed up in my mind I couldn't get clear what was happening, so I painted myself up and dressed in the flashiest party dress I had. Beyond a shadow of a doubt, I looked like a street walker.

When I told the priest that I was going to California to visit my mother and sister, he said, "Paula, that's interesting. I think I'll be able to come out there also. I've been invited to attend a conference and to be a speaker, so why don't you ask your mother if I can stay there with you?"

When Charlie took me to the plane, he'd made arrangements with the airlines that somebody would pick me up and take me from the plane on a wheelchair, as I was so confused that he was afraid of what I might do. Rather than looking like someone who was going to travel, I looked like I was going to take part in some night club review in Las Vegas.

After I'd gotten off the plane, my mother and sister were embarrassed. I knew it was because of the way I looked. To make matters worse, I thought I'd left my make-up bag on the plane which was now leaving. I created a scene like you wouldn't believe and tried to make them stop the plane. But they seemed to ignore me and just took me home and put me to bed.

I lay there for awhile, and I heard the noise of someone getting a drink. I knew they weren't fooling me, so I got up and said, "O.K., make me one."

My mother replied, "Oh, well, you might as well."

All of us got skunked out of our minds. It was so strange to see mother drinking. That was something that happened only after her divorce. In the midst of all the drinking I had enough presence of mind to tell her that the priest would be coming, and I asked if he could stay with us.

Mother had met him and liked him and said, "Sure, Paula. He's such a fine man." My sister seemed interested in meeting him also but had to fly home. I couldn't go to the airport because I was still in bed. Mother went to the airport, picked him up, and brought him home.

Mother went to work the next day, so I was left alone with the priest. There was a little balcony, and I decided it would do me good to take a sun bath.

I put on my bathing suit and stretched out on the deck. It wasn't long until the priest came and sat down beside me. He began telling me what nice legs I had, my figure was so nice, etc., etc. I enjoyed it. I needed to be admired and recognized. Before I knew it, he'd leaned down and kissed me. Yes, I'll have to admit that I felt guilty, but I really enjoyed it, and it excited me. As I was thinking these thoughts of him being in love with me, he said, "Paula, I'm so sorry. I shouldn't have done that."

Of course, I never told anybody, but all night long I couldn't wait for the sun to come up the next morning so that I could take another sun bath. I was really anxious to get on the deck so that he could come and kiss me—which he did.

That night we were all going to go to San Francisco and do the town, hit the bars, and see the flash and fury of that city of sin. I'd never seen anything like it, and living in the small town, I was protected from anything so blatantly evil. We decided we'd all go to a burlesque show. When we got there, I was so embarrassed I didn't think I could stand it. It was a completely nude review. The priest seemed to be enjoying every minute of it.

Suddenly mother said, "Paula, come with me to the ladies room." When the door closed behind us, she said, "I want to talk to you. Paula, that priest is after you, and he means business."

"Mother, he's a priest."

"Paula, now listen to me. I don't care if he is a priest. He's a man, and he's after you, and if you don't do something, you are going to destroy your marriage with Charlie."

"Mother," I said, realizing deep within me that I knew she was right, "you are just imagining all this, and I can handle it. Quit worrying about it."

I stayed in California a few more days and then returned to Shreveport. I began to realize everything mother said was true and that I was really heading for trouble.

Several nights after I returned, my sisters were at the house, the priest was there, and we were all drinking pretty heavily. Lin was there at the time; she was now one of the most beautiful women I'd ever laid eyes on, and when the priest saw her, he took a double flip. I could tell just by looking into his eyes. I wasn't aware of it, but they were trying to dump me, and they were really keeping my glass full. It wasn't long until I was so drunk I could barely stagger to bed. Long before this Charlie had gone to bed. By this time in our marriage he couldn't have cared less. He'd given up on the marriage and everything else.

Several hours had gone by when I woke up, went to the door of the living room, and saw the priest and my sister kissing. It was all right for him to kiss me, but I wasn't going to stand for this man of God to be kissing my sister. Instantly I saw him for what he was. If he was a man of God, he was a fallen man of God.

I started screaming. "Get out of here! Get out of here!" His face turned the color of ashes. My sister and I started fighting like cats and dogs, and I couldn't stop yelling.

Lin ran in and woke up Charlie. She didn't tell him the whole story, and when he came into the living room, he thought I had gone crazy, and he threatened to take me to the ninth floor. He was mad. He was so mad that he struck me (he had never done that before) and disgustingly ordered both of us to bed.

I screamed at my sister over and over, "I never want to see you again." This was the sister I loved so much. My screaming of threats frightened the priest because within a few days he resigned and took up a pastorate in another city. That was the last time I saw him.

The fiasco with the priest had gone on for about a year. It nearly destroyed Charlie and me, and nearly our daughter, Karen. Of course, Karen would come home and see me and the priest drinking—drunk as a kook—and all this time I couldn't understand why she didn't like the nice man, the priest. I could see the hurt in her eyes, but I could not understand why.

I knew deep within that I needed help. I tried everything I could think of. I'd call the toll free numbers which came in the mail from various ministries across the country. They offered to help or take prayer requests, and I certainly needed help. Most of the time I would call after I was full of pills and liquor when it was even hard for me to speak clearly. I would try my best to pour out my heart full of troubles—problems without solutions. Often the telephone counselors would listen for awhile, then try to counsel me and pray, but eventually they would say, "I'm sorry. Your time is up." They would finally hang up on me.

I'd also call different members of the family thinking that somehow one of them would have an answer to my problem. It was so frustrating to them, I'm sure, because they could hardly understand my drug mumble, and I was presenting them with numerable problems that they had no idea how to solve.

It wasn't long until all I would have to say was, "It's Paula," and I would hear the phone quietly go silent, only to dial them back, pleading and begging them, sometimes screaming for them to help me.

I would sit there devastated, lonely, ashamed, hurting, and crying. It broke my heart that apparently nobody in the world really cared for me or could help me.

I went from doctor to doctor to where I would have boxes of pills that numbered into the hundreds. It was unbelievable the collection I had. I'd convinced myself that I needed to take each of them on a schedule. My only problem was I could never remember what pill I had taken. It resulted in overdose after overdose after overdose. I'm sure many of the pills would have been good if I would have taken them properly, but all together I was out of it. The pills turned me into some sort of weird monster who was unpleasant to be around, obnoxious, and slow thinking.

My brother, Douglas, who has always been a precious, sweet person and, I suppose, the sanest one of the family, called and wanted all of us to get together at his house in Kentucky for the holidays—everyone would be there. He'd married a girl by the name of Marie, who everybody knew was a Christian. She was different. She frightened me somewhat, but I felt she had found an answer to life.

It was a long drive from Shreveport to Kentucky, but Charlie thought it would do me good to spend the holidays with my brother because I loved him so much. He thought perhaps there would be an answer there. I packed my bag full of clothes, another bag full of pills, and as we were driving along, I became more concerned and worried that I wouldn't appear right when I saw Doug, so I started popping this pill for my nerves and this pill for this and this pill for that; the closer we got, the more pills I had taken. When we finally reached Henderson, Kentucky, where Doug lived, I told Charlie that he simply had to stop at a gas station because I wanted to fix myself up before my brother saw me. I wanted to look my very, very best for Doug.

I went into the rest room and looked at my face in the mirror. I was shocked at what I saw. I started putting on the mascara and the eye makeup. Nothing seemed to make me pretty. The more I put on, the more disgusting I looked. Then I would put on more, trying to cover that. The next thing I knew I looked like a clown; I was black everywhere. My cheeks were black and my eyes were black. I had smeared makeup from one end to the other. My hands were so shaky, and I couldn't stand what I was looking at. I knew that I could not walk out of that rest room door.

After waiting in the car with the kids for almost an hour, Charlie, in desperation, finally went to the gas station attendant and got the key and pulled me out. I screamed and cried because he wouldn't let me finish putting on my makeup so I could be pretty for Doug. He stood there looking at me in total disgust. He tried to wipe the excessive makeup off my face but with little success. I looked a mess.

When we finally reached Doug's house, the first thing I did was fall down.

"Charlie," Doug asked, "what in the world is wrong with Paula? What's wrong with her, Charlie?"

"Doug, it's the pills. She's not drunk. It's those crazy pills that she eats like candy," he answered.

I was totally embarrassed. I didn't want anyone talking about me. I wanted to have fun. I wanted to enjoy Christmas to its fullest. I wanted to be a carefree child again and eat cookies and candy and pumpkin pie and turkey. It was Christmas. It was a time to have fun—not to be serious—this was party time.

As much as I tried, I couldn't hide that I was in trouble. I could see on every face and in every eye total disgust. I went upstairs and cleaned up, put on a new pant suit, and took some more pills, and some more pills, and some more pills to where even I knew I had taken too many.

Then I heard the voice of my sister, Margaret, downstairs. I could hardly wait to see her. It had been three years since I had seen her—my sophisticated society sister from Louisville!

It was Christmas Eve, and the pills were all mixed up inside me, acting and reacting, working together against my body. How

I tried and struggled to the stairs to see Margaret, but I could scarcely stand, much less walk down the stairs. I was determined I was going to see Margaret. I started crawling on my hands and knees down the hall and then crawling down the stairs. The last thing I remember I was looking down the stairs and seeing Margaret and Doug looking at me, and I said, "Doug, my God, oh my God!"

The next thing I knew it was Christmas, and I was in the hospital screaming. I didn't know where I was or what had happened, but I knew it was my birthday, so I started screaming, "Happy birthday, Paula. Happy birthday, Paula." Then I looked up and saw Charlie. He had put me there. This wasn't the ninth floor, but I knew it was a place in which I shouldn't be. My stomach felt strange, and my throat as though someone was choking me. I screamed and hit at the doctor, asking, "What town am I in? Where am I?"

I might be little in stature, but I have a loud mouth when I start screaming. When another doctor came in the room, I started cussing and blaming him. They all tried to talk with me and reason with me, but no one could calm me. I screamed for them to get my brother. I jumped out of the bed and walked barefooted down into the lobby—torn clothes and all. I looked a mess—like a girl who'd slept on the streets of skid row for a month—and I didn't even care.

I'll never forget the eyes of my brother. He had such a look of despair in his face as he saw me walking across the lobby. The people were looking at me. I was holding my clothes together. I didn't have a coat. I just thought to myself as I looked at the various people in the lobby, *Who do you think you are? Go ahead and look.*

When we returned to the house, I saw Tommy, Karen, and Margaret standing in the foyer. They looked at me and then quickly looked down. They were ashamed and seemed so distant and cool, and that hurt me.

I had always wanted to be like Margaret—so calm, sophisticated. I was sure that now she was sorry I was her sister, or at least that's what I thought.

The beautiful Christmas dinner was now ready to be served. It looked good. It was a table fit for a king, and I hadn't eaten for three days. But I was trembling and shaking so much that I could not manage to get the food on the fork to my mouth. I tried desperately. The food dropped from my fork, and I made a mess on the table. Then my world crumbled as Margaret looked at me and said, "Paula, you disgust me."

I got up from the table, ran to the bathroom, slammed the door, fell prostrate on the floor, screaming and screaming, "God, why me? Don't you love me? I know You are there. Where is the Babe of Bethlehem? Where is the joy of Christmas? Where is the 'joy to the world; the Lord has come'? I don't feel it. If You are there, why can't You help me?"

My brother heard me screaming. He came bursting into the bathroom. Oh, how he tried to love me, but I couldn't accept his love. I thought he just felt sorry for me. Yet in my plea, in my cry, I said over and over, "Please, God, let somebody love me."

By now my imagination ran rampant. The world was against me. My children were against me. Charlie was against me. I knew now that nobody loved me. Everyone was rejecting me. And if anyone even seemed to treat me nice, I would just cry. Oh, how I wanted to go dancing. I wanted to go and do things, but everyone was ashamed to take me along because every place I would go, I would make a fool of myself.

Our trip to Kentucky seemed to be the final straw, and I could tell when we got home that Charlie was thoroughly disgusted with me and wanted to end the marriage. He was trapped, and, of course, he didn't know what to do with me—no one did! I was almost totally bedfast now—addicted, drinking, depressed— and our marriage for all intent and purpose was over. I hated Charlie with a passion, and I knew he hated me. He hardly ever spoke to me, but I knew he was thinking, *How can I get out of this mess?* He couldn't run off, and he couldn't leave. He had a problem that he didn't know how to solve.

Doug had called daddy and told him what a pitiful condition

I was in and about the entire fiasco at his home on Christmas. I tried to keep all of this from daddy over the years, and when he would come to visit me, which was quite frequent when he was working in nearby Magnolia, Arkansas, I would do my best to behave myself. He would bring his bottle in. I wouldn't take a drop because I never wanted my father to see me even shake.

One night he got me alone, sat me on his lap, as he always did when he wanted to talk intimately, and told me about everything he had done. I already knew most of it. He recalled the days when the sheriff was always after him, the trap doors in the house, the moonshine still, everything but murder, but they could never catch him. He began to cry. He could really be tenderhearted at times, and the cry of his heart was that his children would never be like him. He was in torment because he knew how unhappy I was.

Because of Doug's call, daddy came. He had just buried his only brother, Carmen, which seemed to hurt him so deeply. It was as though everybody was gone out of my father's life. He never once condemned me, but got serious and said, "Paula, baby, you are going to lose everything you have. Everything! Charlie's just like I was, honey, and you're going to lose him. Baby, when I lost your mother, the only thing I ever loved, I lost, and you know how much I loved her. I always will. In fact, one of these days I'm going to get her back if that's the last thing I do. She's just so independent. If she hadn't been so independent, we could have made it. Paula, baby, she's the only one I ever loved. I would do anything in the world for all of you kids, but I feel like I've lost each of you."

Tears were rolling down his cheeks as he continued. "You know Carmen. He got his life together when Kitty went to the sanitarium, and you know how her life changed when she found Jesus. Remember when she went to that church and the people reached out and helped her? Honey, that can happen to you, too. And if you don't change, Charlie will take those kids away from you. Don't let that happen, baby."

"Oh, daddy," I cried, "please don't let them take away my

children. Please help me. Help me, daddy. Please, daddy, help me."

"Paula, baby," daddy said, with the tears continuing down his cheeks, "baby, it's only Jesus. Jesus Christ is the only One who will ever be able to help you."

"What do you mean, daddy, when you said you couldn't help me? What are you trying to tell me?"

"That's right, honey, it's only the good Lord who can help you."

"But daddy," I continued, "you know I go to church. You know I go to that old church with Charlie every Sunday. Daddy, it's dead. The music is dead; the sermons are dead. Everything's dead. Charlie just sits around and doesn't want to do anything. My life's empty. It's nothing."

Deep down I knew the torment my daddy was in—because I was there also. I knew exactly the way he felt, the complete hopelessness, helplessness. I didn't feel there was ever a way to have a new beginning, and I heard my daddy say, "Honey, God can do something for you. When Carmen died last week, I talked to the Lord, and He heard me. You know what I've done—I've committed almost every sin and broken every commandment except murder, and I would have done that, but I suppose the good Lord kept me from it. Jesus Christ has now forgiven me of every sin I've committed, and He can help you too, baby."

I'd never heard daddy talk like this. It frightened me and I thought, *Why is daddy telling me all of this?* As I sat there, I had a picture flash across my mind, and I saw him in a casket. But I quickly put it out of my mind. I thought of daddy as a strong man, building houses. He was always a good worker. Then again I came back to reality, and I could tell daddy was restless.

As he was talking, he wept, and we cried in each other's arms. He said, "Baby, please don't do this to me. Go to church. Paula, baby, you've got to let the Lord help you." Then all of a sudden he said, "Paula, let's go shopping." He wanted to get me a new party dress and some high-heeled shoes. He wanted to get Karen some too. He just bought and bought and bought.

Karen was just a little girl, and as soon as we got home, he wanted her to put on the new shoes and the new clothes. She couldn't understand her granddaddy. He wanted to hold her and to love her and be reassured that she loved him, even as he did when we children were little. He'd say to her, "How much do you love me?"

All she'd say was, "Please put me down, granddaddy. Please put me down."

The next morning I knew something was wrong because daddy wanted to leave right away. I pleaded with him, "Daddy, won't you stay tonight?" But he left. I had such a feeling of emptiness when he was gone. I didn't know why I felt this way.

Two days later I got a call from his new wife who said, "Paula, your father is in the hospital." I went to pieces and screamed that we'd be right there. I got Charlie, Karen, and Tommy and immediately went to the hospital.

When I walked in, tears were streaming down his face. He looked at me and said, "Baby, what are you doing here?"

"Well, we've come to see you. We heard you were in the hospital."

"Well, look here, baby. Look at my side. It's all swollen. Look where the doctors have marked off where they are going to take X-rays tomorrow. They haven't said what it is, but let's not talk about me any more."

So we talked empty talk, and I finally said, "Daddy, I called Doug and Margaret, and they are going to come."

He looked at me with such surprise in his eyes. He said, "Paula, what for?" It seemed to frighten him.

"They just want to see you."

Then he said, "You all go and get a motel."

"Daddy, I want to stay with you tonight."

"No, I just don't want you to. There's no need to. I'm all right."

He walked down the hall that evening and had a cigarette because he couldn't smoke in the room. He acted very strong. Then he told me that he wanted all of us to go over to his home, "You have big mama cook your breakfast. I just bought a ham, and I want her to cook that."

I said, "Daddy, we don't want to go over there. We'll go out and eat."

But he insisted, "I told her to cook breakfast."

Hesitatingly we all agreed. We knew we had to go ahead and do what he said.

When we got back to the hospital the next morning, the first thing he asked was, "Now did you go and have breakfast with big mama?"

"Yes."

"That's fine. I want her to give my baby food. I want her to cook for you. You know, baby, I didn't sleep a wink last night. They gave me all kinds of pills, but I couldn't even sleep a wink."

I looked down and saw his tray with all the food on it. I begged, "Daddy, I wish you'd try to eat."

"Leave me alone," he said, but I got the tray and fed it to him anyway. Then I got a comb and started combing his hair. I loved to pet him and comb his hair.

He looked at me and asked, "You still my baby?"

"Yeah, daddy. You want to walk down the hall with me and smoke a cigarette?"

"I don't think I do, baby. I'm just too weak this morning."

"Daddy, Margaret and Doug will be here this afternoon."

He looked at me teary-eyed and said, "I wish they would hurry up."

I wonder why he's saying that, I thought. No one had seen the doctor.

He said, "Well, don't worry about it. I'll know in a little while what's wrong." He thought he had something wrong with his liver because he had drunk so much liquor. Now he was talking about mama. It seemed so strange. He told how he wanted to please her. He commented, "Baby, I've changed. I'm a new man now."

Margaret and Doug were soon there, and he was very happy to see them. Lin couldn't come because she was with mother in California who had just recently had back surgery. It was a touching scene to see daddy hugging and loving Margaret and Doug. Of course, Doug was his only son, so he really looked up to him.

About thirty minutes after they arrived, he sat up in bed and went into terrible convulsions. I screamed, "Daddy, quit that. What are you doing?"

He looked at me and cried, "Help!" That was the last word he said. He seemed to be reaching for God. None of us knew what to do; we were all screaming and running up and down the halls trying to get somebody to help us.

The nurse called the doctor. It was over an hour before he came. The doctor could get no response out of my father. He finally gave him a shot, and he quieted. We stayed with him all night, and his breathing became worse and worse. I knew it was serious. I went to him many times and tried to force open his eyes. Phyllis would say, "Paula, quit doing that," but I'd say, "I want to talk to him. I want him to see me."

We called Lin in California, and she screamed, "Don't let my daddy die! Don't you dare let my daddy die!" She repeated over and over, "I love him. I love him. I love him. Don't let anything happen to him."

He seemed so strong, but he never came out of the coma. The doctor suggested that we take him to Shreveport to a larger hospital. I couldn't bear to be apart from dad, so I rode in the ambulance. We got to the hospital, and the doctor examined him and asked, "Is there anybody in your family that's not here?"

"Yes, my sister. Why, what's wrong?" I questioned.

"Get her here. Your father is dying."

I looked at him and started screaming, "He's not dying!"

"The cancer is all over his body, and it's now taken over his brain," he replied.

Lin didn't know what to do. None of us knew what to do. We had no hope, no resources, no one to turn to. Daddy was now in intensive care. Even though I knew he couldn't hear me, I went in and said, "Daddy, this is baby," and I talked to him and told him I loved him.

Charlie took me home, and Doug went in to be with daddy. When I got back to the hospital, the family was standing by the elevator. When I looked into all those faces, I knew that he was gone. It was as though my whole world ended. When I got home, I fell to my knees. They came and got me up and said, "Paula's on her knees. She's probably on her pills." I had not taken one pill. I was determined to show them that I would NOT take a pill—that I could go through this. I knew they were all sneaking tranquilizers to calm themselves down.

I was so happy when Aunt Kitty came. She was Uncle Carmen's widow. Because she was a very strong Christian, I leaned on her for strength and support. The McGarrh children could see something special in her. Her influence would someday bear dividends.

We took daddy back to the hills where he was born. When he died, I didn't even tell my next-door neighbors, or any of the neighbors, or what few friends we had. I didn't think anybody cared. I didn't call my pastor, even though Charlie was a deacon and treasurer in our church. The loss was traumatic and personal. I was afraid that if someone knew, they would come around and try to perk me up, and worse yet, that perhaps no one even cared.

With daddy dead I felt completely lost. He had been my prop to lean on and had always been around when I needed him. Now he was gone forever.

Daddy had been a very troubled man, but I had some wonderful memories. Physically he was a strong man. I never heard him say, "I have a headache," or "I'm tired," or "I don't feel good." Even on his death bed he didn't complain. He thought he had cirrhosis of the liver—a swollen liver was the first symptom that appeared. He said, "Charlie, you'll have to get yourself another drinking buddy. I won't ever be able to drink with you again." Just a few days later, massive strokes ended his life.

When my life had hit rock bottom, daddy had moved to Shreveport to work. He wanted to be near me so that he could look after me. He was a carpenter and there was plenty of work. On Friday afternoon when he got paid, he would bring his pay to me. "Hold this for me, baby. Don't let me have it if I ask you. I don't want to get in a crap game and lose it all," he would say.

I never held it much past Saturday noon. Gambling was illegal, but there was a game in the bar on Seventieth Street running wide open. Daddy used every excuse in the book to get his money back to get in the game. "Let me have my money, honey," he would say; "I want to go buy you a pair of shoes." I knew just how long I could hold out on him.

All my married life, he would show up for a visit every so often. When he came, he never failed to check my oven to see if "Charlie had cleaned it" lately. As far as he was concerned, cleaning the oven (and the entire kitchen, for that matter) was a husband's job. He was especially irritated at a collection of empty Coke bottles around the house. Tough guy that he was, he never felt above doing housework. He could make the best biscuits you ever tasted. He was an early riser and often cooked breakfast for the family.

Daddy knew Charlie's shortcomings, but they were always good friends. He felt that maybe Charlie would work out eventually. The most important thing to him was that Charlie took good care of his little girl.

When I told Daddy that Tommy didn't like to see him drink, it really hurt him, and he tried to hide it. One Saturday we noticed that Daddy wasn't drinking, but he was making frequent trips to the bathroom. With each trip he came back a little happier. He winked at us and remarked, "Just a little kidney trouble." He was wearing that familiar little smirk on his face.

Tommy found the bottle hidden in the bathroom, and the jig was up. But Tommy always loved and respected his granddaddy very much, and they had many long discussions. Daddy wanted Tommy to be a lawyer. "You know, I may need a lawyer now and then." When he got sick, he said, "Tommy, you'd better be a doctor. I don't think I'm going to need a lawyer."

It was all so futile. I was already programmed for gloom and failure. When the children would leave for school, I would just sink into emotional shock and cry all day. The depression was worse than before.

Suddenly, like a morning sunrise pushing up over the clouds, a bright idea popped into my head. It took the shape of a little round baby face. I wanted a baby! My children were almost grown—Tommy was eighteen years old and Karen thirteen. Wanting a baby was the dumbest thing I ever thought of. "My husband hates me and I hate him. I have incurable diseases, and I don't carry babies very well. I've lost one baby and doctors have told me I shouldn't have any more. Worst of all, I'm thirty-seven years old!" I tried to talk myself out of it. In looking back, I can see that God was the source of that idea.

Two weeks after daddy died, I became pregnant. There was something special about this pregnancy all the way. I breezed through without the customary sickness. The symptoms of Raynaud's disease disappeared, and the diverticulitis was inactive the whole time. I didn't need any medication and didn't have to go to bed. The depression was gone!

When our beautiful little Kelly was born, she seemed special, too. She was—and is—an anointed one. Somebody up there liked us, I decided. But as soon as she was born, the depression came back. My ailments returned worse than ever.

Charlie didn't trust me to take care of Kelly. He got up for the night feedings, saw to her formula preparation, gave her baths, and gave her vitamins. When she needed to go to the doctor, he took her. He even had Dr. Jobe up at three A.M. one night when Kelly developed a slight reaction to some medication. He and Mary Jobe, who was her husband's office nurse, had friendly arguments about the proper way to hold the baby.

I sank deeper and deeper into depression. The self esteem that had come from producing a beautiful baby was wiped out. I was drinking more and more. Charlie joined me. I guess he thought it was the only way we could be compatible.

7
Hidden Treasure

Almost all of the family came to our house that Thanksgiving. Daddy had been gone less than two years, and the hurt was still very real to all of us. We especially missed him at a time like that.

For some reason, nobody was drinking. Usually, there was a lot of booze of some kind, and before it was over, somebody would get ugly about something. But this time there was just conversation, food, and fellowship.

Lin was divorced and had brought her fiancé. She got bored with the talk of football, miniskirts, Nixon, and the price of eggs. She brought out an Ouija board from somewhere and recruited mama to play with her. Lin and mama had always been interested in ESP, horoscopes, fortune tellers, and such. But they had never taken the Ouija board seriously.

Years before, when Lin had lived with us in Baton Rouge, she had played the Ouija with the maid next door. The board had answered questions with uncanny accuracy.

"Are you moving that pointer, Mary?" Lin had asked an unnecessary question.

"No, but you is!" came the firm reply.

Mary was not about to admit that some unseen power was moving the pointer around the board, pointing out letters, numbers, "yes," or "no," in answer to questions of the players.

Mama and Lin stole away to a back bedroom to amuse themselves with the "harmless" game. After asking the Ouija board some questions on different subjects of little importance, something put an idea into Lin's mind. She would later acknowledge that it was a brainchild of Satan!

"Mother! Why don't we try to conjure up daddy with this thing?"

Mama hesitated. There was something about it that didn't sit well with her. She had gone through hell with daddy, and he had been married to someone else at the time of his death. Still, she tried to be understanding of our affection for him and readily joined in our conversations centering on him. She realized that something precious is taken from sons and daughters if they are not allowed to enjoy, and exaggerate, memories from their growing-up days. She finally agreed to take part. Mama and Lin now came to where the rest of the crowd was seated.

This time, when Lin and mama put their fingertips on the Ouija board pointer, the entire atmosphere changed. There seemed to be a presence in the room. The pointer took on power. An energy from somewhere began to make it move, sometimes violently!

The answer came from the Ouija board. "Yes, you can talk with your father."

Lin shivered and mama started to cry. They hadn't meant to activate anything spooky! But it was evident that something was going on, something very evil!

"Daddy, where are you?"

"I'm at peace," came the answer.

"Are you happy?"

"Yes, but I miss all of you. Tell Juanita I love her."

Mama (Juanita) was crying harder now.

Various questions were put to the board, and fitting answers came right back, spelled out faster than we could think! One person stood by with paper and pen so we wouldn't miss a letter.

Lin seemed shocked at all the accurate information being dispensed by the "innocent" little game board she had toyed with so many times in the past. She recalled later that it was at the moment she had opened a channel of thought concerning the spirit of a dead man that the thing suddenly seemed to take on a personality. She believes that a demon which had indwelt daddy, or a spirit that was familiar with him and his surrounding circumstances, entered our presence at this invitation.

Whatever the explanation, it is true that Lin changed that night. She became tormented and mean. In looking back, she is convinced that a demon entered her as they "played the game." According to the Scriptures, this is very likely. God's Word makes it very plain that these things are an abomination to the Lord. "When you enter the land the Lord your God is giving you, do not learn to imitate the detestable ways of the nations there. Let no one be found among you . . . who practices divination or sorcery, interprets omens, engages in witchcraft, or casts spells, or who is a medium or spiritist who consults with the dead. Anyone who does these things is detestable to the Lord" (Deuteronomy 18:9-12, NIV).

But, of course, we didn't know much about the Lord or what He said in His Word. And we didn't pay much attention to the one among us who had been brought up under godly teaching.

When Doug's wife, Marie, heard what was going on, she came out of her seat! She was very upset when she said, "Doug! don't you get involved in that evil mess! I'm warning you!"

But it was too late. Doug had been very close to daddy. He was captivated by the possibility of "talking with daddy." All of us children were.

Charlie, Marie, and the children kept a distance from us. They were frightened with what was going on.

The room was filled with a tension and expectancy. There was fear, excitement, joy, grief, all mixed together. You could have cut the air with a knife. Evil filled the room. We were all crying.

"Tell daddy I had a baby since he died, a little girl named Kelly," I said to Lin, with the air of someone sending a Western Union telegram to outer space.

"Should I marry Barry? Will he make me happy?" Lin asked, hoping for a positive answer. The answer was yes. From what we learned later of the Word of God, this should have been recognized as a prophecy of failure for that marriage.

We went on for three hours, asking questions and holding our breath until the answer came. The air was cold and clammy, even though the thermostat had not been changed. We all had "goose bumps," and mama started boohooing after the thing said that daddy still loved her.

The biggest shock wave came when the board said that daddy had left us some money! That got EVERYBODY'S attention.

Cary McGarrh had made a lot of money, and there wasn't one of his kids who wouldn't have been glad to be mentioned in his will. But there had been no will, no money, no property, nothing. He had owned a beautiful farm with a fine herd of cattle a few years earlier. But, as far as we knew, it was all gone before he died. Cary the gambler, Cary the bootlegger, and Cary the father who loved his family—they were all the same person. Yet, when it came to the end of life, he had neither family nor a token to leave them. His life was so well described in Proverbs 23:29-30: "Who hath woe? Who hath babbling? Who hath wounds without cause? Who hath redness of eyes? They that tarry long at the wine," and in Proverbs 20:1: "Wine is a mocker, strong drink is raging, and whosoever is deceived thereby is not wise."

As the Ouija pointer moved about the board to the different

letters, the words formed were spoken in unison by the interested onlookers. When the message was formed that daddy had left his money in a mattress, four assorted pairs of blue eyes grew to the size of half dollars! I felt the hair rise on my arm, and Lin clutched at my hand as mama and Doug spoke in whispers.

"Would you look at that!"

"Well, what do you think about that?!"

"I knew it! I knew daddy would have some money somewhere!"

The Ouija kept moving. It was spelling out the name of the town in Arkansas where daddy had been living at the time of his fatal illness. M-a-g-n-o-l-i-a.

We managed to wait until morning before running off to look for the hidden treasure. We felt a little foolish, but that didn't stop us. We drove to Magnolia to locate the house and get that mattress. When we got there, we discovered that all of the furniture had been moved out and we would never find it. If there had been any money, it was now lost forever.

All the way home we gave our opinions as to the veracity of the Ouija board.

"I never did believe in that thing. It was foolish for us to drive all that way looking for money because of that silly board!"

"Then tell me, how did that board answer all those questions? Some of them had to come from another world."

"Where do you think the money is now?"

"Do you believe there was ever any money hidden?"

On and on it went. We explored many possibilities.

However, a disaster far worse than the loss of a possible inheritance was now happening. We didn't realize until many years later that I and beautiful, restless Lin were being lured into the web of a sly enemy. Like the clever spider that spins strong but silky strands of invisible bondage, the enemy, Satan, was weaving a trap for us. And we were like dumb flies—heading straight for the trap!

Not mama! She had loved the Lord and often read the Bible. She still had a desire to live for Him.

Not Doug! He had someone—Marie—claiming the blood of Jesus over the doorposts of his home and heart every morning. He would soon become an answer to Marie's prayers—a newborn babe in the family of God, washed in the blood and baptized in the Spirit! If that hadn't happened, I probably wouldn't be here to tell this story.

But Lin and I were easy marks for oppressive spirits wandering about, seeking a habitation. There were manifested evidences of this.

My life went from bad to worse. I had more sickness and misery than ever.

Lin's personality was changed. She experienced seizures of uncontrollable anger more and more frequently. She dabbled in witchcraft and seances, going deeper and deeper into Satan's trap. Though she was small and dainty, when violent anger gripped her, she could slap her 200 pound husband out of his chair!

She soon landed on a psychiatrist's couch, wracked with fears and fantasies. No help would come, though, until the tormenting spirits were cast out.

Few people realize what they are getting into when they play Satan's so-called "harmless" games—fortune tellers at the fair, Ouija boards, horoscopes in the daily newspaper.

We could have avoided all of this misery had we known and utilized the protection God has provided. "Finally, my brethren, be strong in the Lord and in the power of his might. Put on the whole armor of God, that you may be able to stand against the wiles of the devil" (Ephesians 6:10-11). But, instead, we had opened another door to Satan and his evil forces.

8

The Ninth Floor

I could feel life leaving me. I was dying, and I didn't know what to do about it. I was so out of it I couldn't remember one day from the next. I was in constant fear that some day someone would call and say that I had done something terrible and I wouldn't even remember.

Oh, how my Karen and Tommy suffered—Karen especially. Tommy was in college and now hardly came home on weekends. I pretended my children didn't know I was now nothing but a doped-up lush. But they did.

Every day I would lie to the children and pretend I was going to the doctor. Soon it was one lie on top of the other. Then I lost track of what was the truth. I no longer knew.

I was constantly getting my prescriptions filled over and over, ever building a good stockpile of drugs. I was now taking three times the amount of "speed" the doctors had ordered me to take. I was so geared up I was high and flying all day long. Then my nights would become nightmares, never sleeping. Charlie could take no more.

The diverticulitis became worse. I could hardly eat anything. I was down to ninety pounds. One night I decided to get away from it all. I got in the car to race off to who knows where, but Charlie grabbed the keys and restrained me.

My next stop was the psychiatric ward at Schumpert Hospital; the ninth floor. Things must have gotten pretty rough because I woke up with my hands strapped down. My hands were bleeding, and I was screaming at the top of my voice. I lay in torment for four days before a psychiatrist came to see me. I was already in bad enough shape, but it was maddening to watch all the patients walking up and down, up and down, back and forth—going nowhere, with absolutely no purpose. I could only cry. It was a terrible place to be. I thought, "I'm only a day from being like everyone else in this snake pit."

My mind was perfectly clear, but Charlie had left orders that I could not make or receive any phone calls. I pitched a fit one night and told them I was going to start screaming—nonstop—unless they called my husband to come get me. And I could scream loud!

He came, and I was quiet and sweet to him. I held on to him and promised to be good if he would just take me home. I was so desperate I would have made any promise. He promised to come back and get me that night.

Bedtime came, but no Charlie. The nurse wanted to give me a pill to knock me out. I said, "No, my husband will be here any minute to take me home."

But he didn't come. He knew he couldn't do anything with me when he got me home. It broke my heart that he had lied to me. I know that he was hurting almost as much as I.

The next morning I sneaked into the office and called a friend to come get me out. The doctor came in to check on me.

"No, you are not crazy," he told me, "but you had better get a lawyer because your husband wants to keep you on the ninth floor."

"Oh, he does, does he?"

Then it hit me. "Someday if I'm not careful I really *will* be sent to the ninth floor and never get out." I didn't dare say to anyone what I was thinking.

I played it real cool and eventually Charlie did come to take me home. I smiled and purred like a kitten—until I got in the car!

"You _____ ! I'll get even with you if it's the last thing I ever do!" I screamed with all the hate and bitterness I could pour out. "I hate you, you stupid idiot!" On and on I raved as he drove toward home where Karen and little Kelly were waiting for us.

Tears rolled down Charlie's cheeks. That patient man was at the end of his rope, and the desperation and defeat showed on his face. But if he thought things were as bad as they could get, he soon found out differently.

Shortly after the ninth floor experience, an attack of diverticulitis sent me to intensive care. My body was so dehydrated that I came very near dying. I was determined to finish the job this time.

The timing of Satan is right on. Only a few days out of the hospital and one of our old friends was passing through Shreveport and decided to stop in and see us. The next day he was going to Baton Rouge and wanted to know if I would like to ride along and visit Lin.

We had all been drinking, and on the spur of the moment I said yes, and Charlie agreed. I supposed he was glad for the few days of freedom. Charlie hated this man, but he had gone into such a shell that he didn't care any more.

I called Lin and told her I was coming.

We got into the car, and I started drinking and drank most of the way to Baton Rouge. Several times we'd stop a couple of places to drink and dance. When we got there, he said, "Paula, I'm going to check into the motel and then you can call Lin to come and get you." I didn't think that was strange. After all, I'd known this man for years.

When we got to the motel, he kept drinking, but for some reason I quit drinking. I was completely sober. I kept saying, "I've got to call Lin."

"No, you can't call her yet. Paula, let's drink some more. Come on, baby, let's have a little fun."

I kept trying to use the phone, and he would jerk it out of my hand and say, "I told you to wait."

I became terrified and started crying.

He was a very big man. Suddenly he grabbed me and started kissing me.

I screamed, "Leave me alone; stop that!" I knew that now he had lost his faculties. I grabbed the phone to call Lin.

He jerked it out of my hand and again said, "Not now. I told you to wait!" Then he slapped me over and over. No man had ever beat me up. The first thing I knew he was pushing and shoving me to the floor and was raping me. I screamed and screamed.

By this time he had completely turned into an animal. He kept hitting my head against the bathroom floor until I lost consciousness.

When I finally did come to, he was gone. It was horrible. I felt filthy and dirty and didn't know what to do. I felt so degraded, and my stupidity had brought it on. I had such a fear of men anyway; now I was terrified beyond description. I knew I had to get out of there. My head seemed to be bleeding everywhere. I couldn't walk. My face wasn't beat up—just the back of my head —and my arms were bruised all over.

Slowly and cautiously I opened the door to call someone. I was on my knees. A man passed. I screamed, "Help me, please help me!" He just ran.

I returned to the bed and lay there until the maid came to clean the room. She took one look at me and went for the manager. All they wanted was to get me out of there—and fast! They didn't ask any questions. They went through my purse and found Lin's number, and she came and got me.

The next day he had the nerve to call. Lin talked to him. He had told her I was so drunk I had fallen out of the car. No one believed me, not even my sister. With no one believing me, I wanted to go home. I waited several days for my head to heal, and I returned, vowing never to repeat what had just happened.

My mind now seemed to belong to someone else.

I have simply got to kill myself, I thought, *but how?*

Then I remembered Charlie's pistol that he kept in his den. *That's what I will use this time. I can't foul up.*

The children were gone, and Charlie was in the living room. I was trying to think before I moved where the ammunition was. I could remember many times telling Charlie to keep it out of the reach of the children, for I had such a fear of guns. I supposed that came from growing up under the constant threat of violence. I didn't like guns in the house, and I certainly had never touched one. Suddenly there was a smile on my face, and I was so glad that I'd allowed Charlie to have a gun cabinet and his gun collection.

I was full of fear, but soon that fear became nothing as my desperation and the pills and that inner urge within me took over. I snuck into the den where the gun cabinet was. Slowly, deliberately I pulled open the drawer and removed the pistol from its resting place. After a long search I found one bullet that fit in the gun, and I managed to get the pistol loaded. How I accomplished that I'll never know because I knew nothing about guns.

With the gun in my hand I quietly went to the bathroom, where I would end it all. I didn't want Charlie to know. As I opened the door, the squeak seemed to pierce the silence that prevailed in the house. As I locked the door behind me, it sounded as though I had dumped a sack of tin cans on the concrete. I stood there for the longest time reflecting what a waste my life had been.

Finally I mustered all the strength that I had to pull the hammer back into firing position. I'd heard tell that people who are always threatening suicide really don't want to succeed. That might be right, but everything within me that moment wanted to succeed. The gun was ready, and I looked at the woman in the mirror. It wasn't me. I stood there glaring, staring at her with all the contempt that I could muster—boiling and raging inside of me.

Then a voice seemed to speak to me out of nowhere saying, "Kill that woman. Kill that woman."

I looked at her and screamed, "I hate you! I hate you! You've given me nothing but torment and anguish and bitterness, sickness and misery. No one loves me; everyone hates me, and it's all your fault. My family hates me. My husband hates me. My marriage is falling apart. I have no relationship with God or anyone else, and it's all your fault. I'm going to kill you." At that I swung the gun up, and, holding it with both hands, I fired point blank at that woman in the mirror.

The explosion reverberated off the tile walls in the bathroom, and the shock and recoil of the gun knocked me off my feet. I fell to the floor thinking that any moment I would be forever destined in eternity, and God only knew where. But I knew at this point in my life I was in living hell, and I couldn't care less if it were hell for eternity. I'd never had peace except perhaps when I was holding my babies, and that was the only time I felt that I received love. I suppose there were times that I did have fun and a little happiness, but it was so fleeting I could hardly remember.

I lay there stunned and dazed, and then I was brought back to the starkness of reality that again I had failed. I heard the shout and clamor of Charlie beating on the door screaming, "Paula, Paula, Paula."

All I could think was, *Oh, my God, I failed again. There's Charlie.*

At that moment he came bursting through the broken door. I'll never forget the look in his eyes as he bent over me. They reflected rage and hate and disbelief and yet relief, I suppose, thinking momentarily I would be dead. I lay there in shock, unhurt. All I could think of was, "I've got to get that mirror fixed."

"Charlie, get that mirror fixed. I don't want anybody, especially the children, to know that I've done this. Charlie, get that ˙rror fixed!"

Glass was splattered everywhere. It was a miracle that my and face and all of me hadn't been cut with the fury of the ˙r of the glass. Now I felt ashamed. I had failed. I had failed!

I couldn't even kill myself.

Charlie picked me up and almost threw me in the bed, and then I heard him call mama in California. I screamed to him, "Don't tell mama. Don't tell mama." But his face was like flint and unemotional. He couldn't care less what I thought.

When mama answered, I heard him say with no emotion, "You've got to come; Paula has tried to kill herself again. I don't know what to do anymore." Poor mama, she didn't know what to do either, but she did come and stay awhile. It was apparent they all thought I would try it again, for she watched me like a hawk. And well she should because I had tried so many times. One time when I took a whole box of sleeping pills, all I had the next day was a headache. I even drank poison, and it didn't burn my tongue or even give me a sore throat. I tried razor blades, and you name it.

Little did I know that "the effective, fervent prayer of a righteous man availeth much," and there were some righteous people praying for me and my family, though I did not know about it.

Through all of this torment and mess God's hand was on me.

Charlie's face reflects utter despair; he had given up hope for a happy marriage.

Inside, I was in turmoil. I tried to look normal, but I had lost my feminine softness.

God has restored our lives and placed His beauty within.

9

Oh Boy, a Party!

For my own protection Charlie again had taken me to the ninth floor, the psychiatric ward. Oh, the torment, the heartache, the fright, the anguish, the loneliness of being in there. Forever I was thinking, *How can I end it all? How can I do it?*

I knew I had to be away from the ward because I was watched too closely. So all that was within me came together and I put on an act, and soon I was released.

One night soon after I'd returned home, I received a call from Doug and Marie in Kentucky, inviting me to come to their home for a visit. My first impulse was to say O.K. Then I remembered hearing that they both had turned into religious fanatics, and I didn't want any part of that, so I backed off by saying, "Doug, I don't think I can handle a visit with you right now."

It was obvious that Doug and Marie both knew how seriously ill I was and that they really wanted me to come. Marie got on the phone and pleaded with me, telling of the great plans they had for Saturday night. "Paula, please come. It will do you so much good —and bring your best party dress!"

A party! I haven't been to a party for months! Charlie is such a stick-in-the-mud and won't let me party anymore. He watches over me. This will be a chance for me to be free. That's just what I need! "Marie, I'll pack my prettiest party dress, and we'll go out on the town. Oh, that will be so much fun. I'll be there, and I'll bring Kelly with me."

Doug was so sweet when he met little Kelly and me at the airport. Tears came into his eyes as he told how wonderful God had been to them and what He had done in their lives.

Instead of listening to what he was saying, my thoughts were, *I don't want anybody sitting around me telling about God, I want to party and drink. I want to have fun.*

Doug excitedly remarked, "Paula, you know that big knot or growth I had on my throat; do you know? God healed it. He took it away! He can do the same miracles in you." Over and over in those first moments in the car Doug kept telling me, "Paula, Jesus can help you. Jesus is your answer."

A lot he knows. Jesus could never help me, I thought.

The Holy Spirit in Doug was reaching out to me, but I certainly wasn't tuned into his frequency. But my brother just kept reaching anyway. I could not figure out what was going on, but I knew it was worse than I had ever imagined. His wife had totally warped his mind. I began wondering if I had made a mistake in going to Kentucky.

Then the thoughts of the party overwhelmed me, and I just couldn't wait. As soon as we got to the house and said our hellos, I started primping. Little did I know that Marie and Doug had about everybody they knew in Kentucky praying for me.

When I asked where we were going, I was told we were going to a Full Gospel Businessmen's party.

"What's that?" I questioned.

"Oh, you'll see. Don't worry about it, Paula. You'll have the best time of your life," answered Doug.

When we arrived at a very nice restaurant, I noticed cars parked everywhere. I had on my brand new coat, and I certainly didn't want anyone to steal it, so I questioned about just hanging it up—like I noticed everybody else did.

"Paula, you can leave your coat here. Nobody will steal it," Doug said.

I thought, "Doug is even so far gone now he's got to the place where he can trust everybody. He's really going to get ripped off one of these days."

Right away I looked around for a waiter or waitress to come and take our drink order. But there were no waitresses. Everyone was going through a food line. The dinner was being served buffet style.

I saw several women walk up to each other, and they actually embraced, but when I saw men coming in and hugging each other I thought, *This is really weird. What kind of place has Doug brought me to?*

After we'd finished the meal, a man stood in front, and everyone started singing songs. I'd never heard anyone sing songs like this. I thought, *What am I doing here? Where am I? What's up?* After listening a bit, I began enjoying the way the people sang. It was so loud and happy. It seemed they were really having fun; they were so full of joy. Then I saw a hand pop up like children in school who needed to be excused to go to the rest room. First one, then another and another. The next thing I knew everybody's hands were raised. I'd never seen anything like it. Then to my amazement my poor brother did it. I felt so embarrassed for him I just looked down at the floor.

I thought to myself, *I'm in pretty bad shape, but they are worse off than I. I'm getting out of this nut house. This must be what you really call Kentucky hillbillies.* I couldn't figure out what all of this had to do with a party in the restaurant. I was confused!

I turned to tell Doug that I was going to the car, but when I looked into his eyes, I saw such love and joy and peace I couldn't speak any words. About that time the man who apparently was in charge introduced, as he said, "a Baptist layman." Well, I'd gone to a Baptist church at one time, so I thought it would be O.K. to listen to him.

He was talking about Jesus Christ. He talked like he knew Him personally, that He was alive, and that he was walking with Him. He looked straight at me and said very distinctly, "Jesus loves you." That really got my attention. Nobody had ever said that to me in such a convincing way.

Shortly thereafter Doug reached over and calmly took my hand. It felt so good and warm, him holding my hand. I slowly turned my head, and my eyes looked at him. I saw tears were coming down both eyes. I was shocked, for Doug was praying out loud and everyone could hear him. I could have died with embarrassment. He said in a very loud and distinct voice, "Jesus, I got her here; now it's up to You."

When he said that, something seemed to pierce through me, and I thought I'd been tricked. I couldn't believe they would do this. I thought we were here for a party, and now my brother had gone crazy. *I don't need help half as much as he needs it. And these people with raised hands, they are so tacky. I feel so embarrassed for all of them.*

I was startled as Marie leaned over and asked, "Paula, don't you want to go up and let that Baptist man pray for you now?"

"Oh, no, Marie, I'm O.K. I'm fine," I answered and got up and started for the door. Instead of making the turn toward the exit, I turned toward the front and found myself standing in front of that man, trying to tell him everything I knew in one breath. But he didn't seem to be listening to my babbling at all. It was as though he knew everything I was going to say. He calmly stretched forth his hand and placed it on my head. It was like electricity went through me; it made me so weak that I fell to the floor. I remember thinking as I was going down, *My goodness, I came up for him to pray for me and all he did was knock me down.*

Then I realized that many around me were standing. I noticed Doug and Marie were crying. I kept trying to get up and thought, *This is ridiculous,* but it was like I was glued to the floor. This was the first time in my life that I'd ever been "drunk" without touching a drop.

People around me seemed to be talking in a strange language, but I felt such a warmth, as though I was being bathed in hot oil. I knew it was love, something I'd never had before. Then someone helped me up, and I assumed the party was over.

"Doug, what on earth happened to me?" I asked.

"Oh, Paula, honey, it was Jesus. It's the new wine. It was just Jesus."

Everything these people were saying was foreign to me. Everyone but me had sensed a miracle had taken place.

When we returned home, I didn't want to go to bed. I wanted to know what all of this was about. Doug and Marie began telling me about the Holy Spirit, which really got my interest.

"What's the Holy Spirit," I questioned; "we sang about it in church, but it never rang a bell. And tell me about this Full Gospel thing; what is it?"

They would give me this Scripture verse and that Scripture verse, and I wrote them down. This went on until three or four in the morning. Then I began wondering, "How on earth am I going to remember all these things? I'm going to forget." But for three days and far into each night they talked about Jesus and the Holy Spirit of God.

I'd noticed I could eat anything and that I felt good. I wasn't weak and I wasn't in bed. I could stay up. I felt great! I had love. I looked in the mirror, and for the first time in my life I loved the person I saw. I felt the presence of God. I knew that God was real. Then I wanted to go home!

I wanted Charlie to hear what had happened. Ah, yes, Charlie! He and I had problems. I said to Marie, "I don't like Charlie at all. I want this marriage to end, and I can't understand what it is in me that wants to call Charlie."

"Oh, Paula, call him. Call him and tell him you love him."

Slowly I walked to the phone. It seemed like an eternity as I dialed the numbers. The click of the phone seemed to mock me; then I heard his "Hello."

"Charlie, I'm coming home." I could hear his sigh of disappointment.

Marie was there egging me on and saying, "Paula, tell him you love him. Tell him you love him."

I hung up and turned to her with, "Oh, Marie, don't be silly. He'll never believe that." Charlie was hardened. He'd lost hope. He was like a walking zombie. I was so amazed at what I'd done to him. One of the main reasons I married him was because of his sweetness and gentleness, and now he seemed so harsh and mean that I couldn't talk to him. He was like another person. I was determined to go home and share with him what had happened.

On my flight back I could smoke or drink, and yet I had no desire for any of it. For the first time in my life I felt a peace. Then I decided I'm not going to tell him much of what happened. This whole business of salvation, healing, being slain in the Spirit, this unknown language, none of it now seemed to scare me, but I was afraid that my quiet, conservative, and intellectual Charlie would put me back on the ninth floor if I would tell him all that happened to me in Kentucky. And I was determined within my heart that I would NEVER go to the ninth floor again.

I got off the plane serenely and quietly. I wasn't off the plane ten minutes until I told him EVERYTHING. He sat there absolutely stunned. He looked at me in horror. I thought, *Oh, God, he's going to drive me to the hospital!*

Then he spoke, "Paula, I sent you to Kentucky to get rid of you. Now you come back in worse shape than when you left—even now talking about this tongues business. Well, at least I hope you'll go to church with me."

Several hours later Charlie did tell me that I looked different. That pleased me.

I wanted everybody to hear what had happened to me. I thought everybody would be happy and thrilled because now I could eat. I was almost normal for the first time, and I felt love coming to me from somewhere.

I went to our pastor and told him what had happened to me. When I finished, he looked at me, saying, "Paula, how could you believe all of this? Don't you know it's just for those emotional and weak simple-minded people?"

"Pastor, but you know you visited me in the hospital and know how sick I was. Now I'm not sick. I can even eat Mexican food. I don't need liquor. I don't need my pills."

"Oh, Paula, you'll be sick next week. This is just an emotional trip you are on. Don't you remember when that woman took off for that charismatic church and how I talked to her trying to convince her not to go. Even you thought she'd taken leave of her senses. Now what do you think people are going to think about you?"

I knew the pastor was a wonderful man. He was always willing to help, and I suppose he really had my welfare at heart, but the words he spoke seemed to be killing that love in me. He seemed to be destroying that song in me. My happiness seemed to be turning into sadness and my victory into defeat. That which I'd found seemed to be slipping from my hands. I didn't know how to keep hold of it. After several weeks I woke up one morning, and I knew I was alone. I had lost what I'd found. I was without guidance or encouragement. Charlie couldn't understand my faith, and I didn't know anyone to talk to.

In a few days I was back in the hospital worse than ever. Every shot and kind of medicine they gave me would have terrible side effects. I went into convulsions. I had strokes and could hardly talk. I tried to tell everyone that the medicine was killing me, but I couldn't talk. Finally I wrote Charlie a note. He thought I was pretending, as I had done so many times before. I really couldn't blame him for feeling that way. However, there was one nurse who believed me and would come into my room at night. I would be there crying. She would take hold of my hand and pray for me.

The doctors finally stopped the medicine. They must have realized what was happening to me because they had me sign a release. I was able to go home a few days after they stopped the medication.

I was told by several doctors that I needed surgery on my colon and also for a hemorrhoidal condition, but they said my condition made it too risky. Charlie and I finally found a well-known surgeon who said he would perform the surgery. "The first thing we'll do," he said, "is deal with the hemorrhoids, and then after you recuperate, we'll take out the diseased portion of your colon. I'm going on vacation for a month, but when I get back, we'll put you in the hospital and begin the surgery."

Mother had developed glaucoma and was hospitalized. Doug went to visit her and shared Christ with her, and she claimed her complete healing. She was not only healed but also "filled with the Holy Spirit." Soon mother was on fire for God with power and zeal like none of us had seen. She became the first "McGarrh" girl to dedicate her life to serving Christ.

10

Coming to Life

During the month the doctor was on vacation, Lin called from Baton Rouge. "I want you and Charlie and the kids to come for the weekend." She sounded excited.

Lin had been in worse condition than I, but in a different way. Here was a girl who had a good job, was a personal friend of the governor, and had everything a girl could want. She was beautiful, had all the clothes she wanted, and her life always seemed to be exciting. But she had been divorced twice and was very unhappy. She had sought satisfaction in alcohol, horoscopes, Ouija boards, seances, and other deceptive devices of witchcraft. She was miserable.

That was before her trip to Kentucky. The same place, the same thing happened to her that happened to me. (I used to wonder if God lived in Kentucky and you had to go there to find Him.)

The first night she had gotten saved, asking Jesus Christ to be the Lord and Savior of her life. The next night they took her back to the meeting, and she started feeling strange, like there was a power coming over her. "I want to get out of here!" she said with a note of desperation.

"No," said Doug.

"Let me OUT!"

"No. Settle down now."

"LET ME OUT OF HERE!" she was screaming by that time. She didn't care about the crowd of people looking at her.

My poor brother. Here he was again with one of his sisters creating a scene.

Norvel Hayes, the businessman speaking that night, rushed to her and took control of the situation. With authority he said, "In the name of Jesus, you come out of her!"

Lin screamed louder. All around her people were praying in tongues, and she thought everybody had gone crazy.

Mr. Hayes explained to the audience. "People, this lady has a problem with satanic forces that have sought to destroy her. Demons frequently gain entrance into our lives when we willingly or unwittingly open the door for them by dabbling in witchcraft or the occult. These evil powers sometimes become so strongly entrenched that our very thought life is taken over, and we are unable to pull down the evil imagination strongholds. The Word of God instructs us to use the name of Jesus and cast these evil spirits out. If you will keep the Word of God in your thought life and spirit, the demonic powers can have no entrance."

Then Lin remembered our fooling around with the Ouija board and fortune tellers and her going to seances and realized that these evils had been in her for a long time, but they had to leave, for she did not want them to destroy her life. After awhile the demonic forces left, and she went limp and was "slain in the spirit" for a long time. When she got up, she was a different person. (Norvel Hayes still occasionally talks about the "beautiful witch.")

So here she was a few weeks later, insisting that we come spend the weekend with her. I told her we were having trouble with our car. She said God could take care of that. We weren't too surprised when, ready to leave, we found that the car was in good working order.

When we arrived, Lin had a crowd of people over. She had already found a church and Spirit-filled young people to fellowship and stand with her. Joe Hurston, later to become Jimmy Swaggart's business manager, was there. He, and others, tried to explain spiritual things to us and then prayed for us. I was in awful pain. They told me the Lord was going to take that pain away. He did.

The Lord was working on Charlie. Lin had some of Norvel Hayes' tapes which fascinated him. He kept listening to one tape over and over. It was titled "God's Power." There was something about the way Norvel expressed it that made it believable for Charlie.

Lin and her friends had told us about their church, Bethany Baptist. Charlie agreed to go, even though they had described it as "a swinging" church. He felt safe because it was called "Baptist."

When we walked into the church, all we could see was people crowded in, everyone singing and *shaking tambourines!* Charlie didn't exactly feel comfortable, but the Lord had him glued to his chair. God was changing our hearts. We went back that night—not stopped by the tambourines or the "dancing in the Spirit."

Someone testified that the Lord had "given" someone a car, and mentioned Life Tabernacle in Shreveport. That was funny! Karen had gone to visit "Life" a few times with her friend, Beverly. She had come home telling me the people at that church all prayed out loud, raised their hands, and she couldn't understand what they were saying to God.

"They do what?" I had yelled. "You are not going there again. You can just bring your friends to our church where people act normal."

The next Sunday after we came back from Baton Rouge,

Charlie asked, "Where do you want to go to church?"

"Let's try that church they mentioned at Bethany, Life Tabernacle."

God truly works in mysterious ways. About a month before this, I had been in bad shape one night. I was real dopey from all the medicine, when I dialed a number and, somehow, got Life Tabernacle. It was just down the road from our house, but I never would have called there on purpose! I had called all over the country, but here at last I had found someone who really seemed to care. I had kept threatening to kill myself, ordering the lady who answered the phone NOT to trace the call, and all kinds of incoherent ramblings.

This lady had listened very patiently, prayed, and read the Bible to me. Then she said, "Now if you ever come out to the Tabernacle, I want to meet you. I play the piano."

I remember thinking, *Big deal! I don't care what you play. You won't ever see me.* Even though I had been nearly stoned, I could remember the love in her voice. (It was Anna Jeanne Price, I learned later.)

When we went to the Tabernacle, I stayed low in my seat so the lady at the piano wouldn't see me. I just knew she would look out in the audience and know it was me. But after the meeting we did make ourselves known to her.

The music was beautiful, and I could feel love there. There was something different about this church. Pastor Jack Moore spoke, and love came across in his voice, too. I couldn't understand all he preached about, and for some strange reason I felt at home. Charlie liked it, too!

We were ready to go back that night.

11

Let George Do It

The very next week after our first visit to Life Tabernacle, the first Charismatic Conference was held at the Civic Theater, and we were right there!

We had heard about the Holy Spirit baptism, and I had passed on to Charlie all I could remember of what Doug and Marie had told me in Kentucky. We had seen enough evidence of the power and love of God in other people's lives to know that we wanted it.

The guest speaker was George Otis, a former Lear Jet executive and "jet setter," now a born-again, Spirit-filled Christian and friend of Pat Boone. He had some tapes for sale at the Civic Theater. One was on how to receive the Holy Spirit. We bought the tape and planned a private do-it-yourself project at home, in quiet dignity. Charlie had come this far, and I didn't want some Kentucky-style scene turning him off. He had been embarrassed too many times by my falling around drunk or drugged. I could imagine what he might do if I (or worse, he) got "slain in the Spirit." I thought about how Lin had been oppressed by a demon, and I knew that if that happened to me, Charlie would be too humiliated to claim me! There was no doubt about it. We needed to find out more about this subject. I had heard about a man in Kentucky commanding the devil to come out of a woman. Maybe Charlie should try that on me, and then I could do the same for him!

We took the tape home, got comfortable, and listened to the whole tape, waiting for something to happen. Nothing did. We just sat there at the kitchen table, looking at each other, wondering why it had to fail on US.

I figured I had gotten something mixed up, or maybe forgotten to tell Charlie some of the details from the Kentucky visit. I thought I remembered an incantation in which they "begged the blood of Jesus." Sometimes hands were placed on heads. Some had seemed to get high by singing, usually starting on a high "Hallelujah." Maybe we ought to sing.

"Why don't you sing 'Hallelujah'?"

"No. I'd feel silly."

Somehow, we just hadn't gotten a clear understanding of how to get Jesus to baptize us. We decided to go back to the Civic Theater and "let George do it."

That night, as the service came to a close, George Otis said that anyone who wanted the baptism in the Holy Spirit should come forward. Charlie and I almost ran down the aisle! I didn't care what it took to get it. If they told me to roll on the floor (we had heard that old tale somewhere) or sit on a dunce stool and stick out my tongue, it didn't matter. I was ready!

We were taken to an area where the stage was packed with "seekers." Mr. Otis, a brilliant scientist-author, explained how easy it would be for everyone there to be baptized in the Holy Spirit, as promised in John 14:16 and Acts 2:38-39 and 11:15-16.

"You don't have to tarry or work for it. It is simply a gift from God, and you reach out by faith and receive it, just as a child takes a present offered to him by a loving parent," he kindly advised us. "Didn't Jesus say, 'If ye then, being evil, know how to give good gifts unto your children; how much more shall your heavenly Father give the Holy Spirit to them that ask him?' "

That was easy enough to understand! As a smile of comprehension started to spread over my face, I looked at Charlie to see if he had caught on, too. But his eyes were closed, and his lips were moving. I seemed to be the only one peeking. I quickly closed my eyes and, with my inner sight, looked to my heavenly Father (or was it my Father which was in heaven—or was it Jesus—or George?). Before I had time to get confused, I held out my hands and said, "Thank You, Lord," and received His gift of peace and joy in the Holy Ghost, which flooded through me and overflowed through the soft, flowing language of the Spirit speaking through me.

By that time, at least fifty others around me were praising and magnifying God with a new tongue. There were people from many different church backgrounds, and some had driven over a hundred miles to be in the meeting.

"Well, we can go now," my sweet husband said.

We walked off the stage and back down the aisle, feeling all warm and wrapped up in the love of God.

I looked at Charlie and thought, *Look here! I got me a brand new husband without even having to get a divorce!* I didn't ask him, but I'm sure Charlie was hoping he had a new wife.

He did. He had a new WIFE and a new LIFE!

Talk about miracles! We had one after the other. I was healed of the terrible diseases that had been almost destroying my body. I had no withdrawal agonies, though I had been on the prescription drugs for years. The Raynaud's disease left, and my features started going back to their normal size. The diverticulitis was healed; I could eat anything I wanted. We didn't need to drink liquor anymore—we had the real joy now. The cigarette craving went slowly, but it went. God restored our marriage, my health, everything!

No one enjoyed church more than we. We had been saved

from a terrible, hopeless situation. It seemed that the pit we were lifted out of was deeper than most. We could hardly wait for time to go to church. Now the songs had meaning, such as:

> *Amazing grace! How sweet the sound!*
> *That saved a wretch like me!*
> *I once was lost, but now am found;*
> *Was blind, but now I see.*

How true those words! When we heard that beautiful, clear voice of Marcelle Scully singing "Higher Ground" or "Fill My Cup," our cup too ran over!

We could say, along with our pastor, Jack Moore, "We've discovered the secret of how to have everything and live forever!"

At that time we had almost reached the point of financial bankruptcy. All the illness and our life style had taken everything we had. We were broke and deeply in debt.

Charlie and Tommy had been involved in a little sideline business with two World War II search lights, doing advertising for grand openings, shopping center sales, etc. Now we needed very badly to sell the equipment, since Tommy would soon graduate from Louisiana Tech and would be moving.

Driving to Baton Route to investigate a sale possibility, the peace of God was very present, in spite of our circumstances.

Charlie expressed our feelings when he said, "You know, it really doesn't matter. Even if we go bankrupt, lose our job, our car, or the equipment, we have Jesus in our lives now, and nobody can take Him away from us!"

We didn't lose anything. We sold the equipment, and very gradually we paid off our debts.

God restored much of what the "canker worm" had eaten away!

The doctor came back from vacation, and I was scheduled for surgery. That night in bed I knew the Lord had touched me and had healed me, and I knew now for certain I was a born-again Christian. I realized that I had been saved in Kentucky, but I just never had the full assurance of what had happened.

As I lay there, I "begged" the blood of Jesus over me. I, of course, couldn't remember the terms. I said, "Lord, in case I really wasn't healed when I was in Baton Rouge, I need a sign or something from You. I'm so confused, and if You want me to have that operation, then when the doctor examines me, let him realize that I need the surgery. He's got this whole thing set up, and he's going to think I'm stupid if I call him and say I don't need surgery anymore. I just simply can't tell him that I've been healed."

I can't understand why I was so foolish to say such a prayer, but I did. When I woke up the next morning, I was in pain. I heard the Lord speak to me and He said, "Paula, because you doubted, you'll have the surgery, but I will not let you suffer."

I was so startled because it was like He spoke to me in an audible voice. Then it hit me, *Oh, no, I'm going to die. That's the reason I'm not going to have pain!* But in spite of all, I had such comfort knowing I was going to die and there would be no pain in my death.

Charlie was supposed to go to New Orleans the next day, and I tried not to talk him out of it. I assured him I was O.K. I went through the operation, woke up, and there was no pain. That morning I started writing my testimony.

As I look back even for a few moments, I was like that fairy tale egg, Humpty Dumpty. I was just all broken and crushed. It seemed impossible to everybody that anybody could ever really put me together again, but God was certainly performing miracles in our lives.

12

A 'Reacher'

My days now were so full of excitement that I could hardly wait to see what the Lord would do that day. My faith was simple and childlike, and absolutely nothing was impossible for my God and Savior.

I recall one morning in particular. I'd fed little Kelly, and she was playing, when all of a sudden I got so weak I could hardly stand up. I had to go to bed. It was one of the strangest feelings I'd ever had, especially after my new experience with Jesus. I didn't know whether I was going to die or understand what was happening to me. As I was lying in the bed, I became aware of a bright light moving toward me. I knew it was the presence of Jesus. I closed my eyes and began weeping and weeping. His presence was overwhelming me. My room was so bright I was afraid to open my eyes, lest it would blind me. Oh, how desperately I wanted to see the Lord, but I could not open them.

I thought, *Jesus is here. He's going to take me home.* Ever since I had become a Christian, I'd heard about the soon return of Jesus, and how I longed for that. People called it the "rapture." I could scarcely remember the word, except that I would fly away as the song said that we had sung so much.

The Lord spoke nothing. Then it was as though He started turning the pain off in my body, beginning with my feet. I couldn't imagine what was happening. *He must be getting me ready to go to heaven,* I thought. I didn't think to talk to Him, everything that was happening felt so good.

Suddenly I felt His hand on my head, and peace overwhelmed me. I thought, *I wish I could tell everybody how beautiful it is to know you are going to be with the Lord. It isn't scarey to die. It's beautiful, wonderful, peaceful and, oh, so serene.*

Then I became concerned about little Kelly, and I spoke. As I spoke, the light left the room, but, oh, the peace remained. I lay there about two hours and thought, *I've got to call Charlie because Jesus may come back and get me. Maybe He was preparing me.*

In my weakness I crawled to the phone and called Charlie. I whispered, "Charlie?"

"What?" he asked.

"Charlie, guess what? The Lord came."

"What? Paula, are you all right?"

"Charlie, Jesus has been here. If I'm not here, you'll know I'm with Him. I love you. Bye."

Needless to say, Charlie was home in fifteen minutes to check on me.

I'll never forget that day. I went to the mailbox, and there was a letter from Oral Roberts. I'd always made fun of him since I was a little girl because I thought he was absolutely a fake. I'd never heard of anyone being healed before, and I didn't believe in anything he had ever done. But when I opened that letter, it began: "Dear Sister Kilpatrick, I feel that the Lord has touched you and made you whole today."

As I read those words, tears welled up in my eyes, because it was true and Jesus had just visited me and He HAD touched me. I thought, *How does he know this?* I'd never written Oral Roberts. To this day I don't know how I got that letter.

I sat in the chair the whole day and read that letter over and over and cried and prayed and cried.

Before Charlie went back to work, he kissed me and kissed me. We were so green and such novices in the Lord, he too thought that maybe I was going to be raptured.

From that day on, every letter that I received from Oral Roberts, mimeographed or whatever, meant much to me. It was years before I understood that he hadn't sat down and personally written, but I kept every letter that he sent me. It was rather funny because I'd call the pastor and tell him that I'd gotten a letter from Oral Roberts, and I asked him if he would like for me to read it to him.

"Is it a personal letter?" he'd ask.

"Sure." And I'd read it to the very end. Nobody wanted to hurt my feelings, but it made no difference because God used every word that was in every letter to bless me. Because of the first letter that day, beyond a shadow of a doubt, I knew that I'd been completely and totally healed of every disease.

Things were so different now. Truly my cup was running over. I knew that life would never be the same again. Love had taken on such a greater meaning. I felt a new love in my heart for Charlie. I even loved myself. Instead of my feeling sorry for myself—*that poor pitiful Paula*—as everyone had called me, I now saw myself as the one bought with that precious price of Jesus. I came to realize more than ever that God loved me—me, Paula Kilpatrick—so much that He sent His only Son Jesus to die for me.

But God certainly wasn't through with me or my family.

Three months had passed, and the church which we were attending had a guest speaker, a Catholic priest named Michael Gaydos. We took Karen to hear him, and it was our prayer that while Michael was at the church that Karen would also receive the Holy Spirit. Sure enough, Michael asked the question if anyone wanted to receive the Spirit, and when Karen lifted her hand, I sobbed and sobbed because the Lord Jesus was now working on the entire family.

Karen had gone through so much in her short life. She saw me crawling around, stoned out of my mind; she saw me teasing the men, but that day HER life changed.

It wasn't long before our tiny little Kelly accepted Jesus.

When Kelly was just four years old, I laid my hand on her, and she received the Holy Spirit. We were all pleasantly surprised the next night when Karen came running into the living room and said, "Mom, dad, you'll never guess what. Kelly is praying in the Spirit."

At that moment little Kelly came in and said, "Yes, and that's not all; I can sing in the Spirit too."

Kelly was always the type who wanted you to pray with her when anything was wrong. And if something was the least wrong with her, I would say, "Well, let me get you an aspirin," and she would say, "No, mama, let's believe God to heal me."

Because she was just four years old, I couldn't figure out how I was going to keep her quiet, for I knew that she was likely to tell everybody what had happened.

The next morning I decided I would tell her, "Kelly, you are not going to go to kindergarten and tell everybody."

She looked at me and said, "But, mother, I know how to tell people because last night Jesus kept me awake talking to me and telling me what it was all about." It's been such a joy to see God permit our little one to move in the gifts of the Spirit.

It was so much fun for us now as a family to sit in the church and be fed spiritually. It was almost like every night I would go out of the church almost drunk as a coot, and Charlie would have to lead me. Our pastor would say, "Well, there's Paula all drunk in the Spirit again." It was so wonderful, and such a joy. I felt so much love from everybody. I wanted to love everybody. I wanted to tell the whole world that Jesus is alive and active and wants to give His children everything.

During this time of intense "feeding" I had my first spiritual dream. I dreamed I was in a bookstore in the church and was clinging to a lady who was going to be a missionary. She was very small in stature, and I kept yelling, screaming at her, "Don't leave me; I can't count."

As I spoke, she disappeared and Jesus was standing there. He said, "Paula, I'll be your light."

When I woke up, I had a deep sensation that that dream was truly from God, for I did not like being responsible to anyone or anything. I'd always been rebellious to Charlie, to my father, or to anybody who wanted to tell me what to do. I had never submitted to anybody.

I was in church, and as I walked by this lady, she said, "Paula, I believe the Lord would have you work in the bookstore with me."

I looked at her in amazement and said, "Hallelujah, praise the Lord!" and walked past her thinking, *Why did I say that; I can't count!* Then I remembered the dream. It swept over me, and I recalled the Lord saying, "I'll be your light."

The next Sunday Charlie began singing in the choir, and on Monday I began working in the bookstore. God had put an awful lot of love in me, and He certainly knew where to put me to receive love. The people of the church were drawn to the bookstore. Nobody cared whether I could count or not, but God was training and teaching me, and He started working through me.

I would be startled because when persons came in, I would know whether they were depressed or whether this one had fear or whether they needed prayer for healing. God began using me, and I became bold as a lion.

Charlie began having feelings of discontentment working at the hospital, and I just couldn't understand that. I thought perhaps it was the devil. Charlie did too. Soon God directed Charlie to go into business for himself and start an accounting firm. Since then I've discovered that when we become unhappy, many times we blame Satan when really it is the Lord trying to get us into His will.

Karen was engaged to a nice young man, Sonny, and I loved him like a son. Many times he had seen me drunk, and as he'd take Karen out on a date, I'd give them orders not to drink because I did not want the children to be like me. I'd now given him the *Living Bible* and many other books. It wasn't long until he found Jesus and was baptized in the Holy Spirit.

One day Karen came home with a new record album. She had heard Ernie Williams sing. He had been singing with his family all over the United States since he was a little boy. He was very talented and wrote many of his own songs. She put on the album, and as she heard him sing, she began crying and then went to the phone and called her fiance and told him that the engagement was off.

I stood there shocked! I wondered, "Why did she do that? He never argued with her, and now it is ended." She had fallen in love with the boy in the record and was determined that he alone would be her husband!

The next weekend we'd gone to visit Charlie's mother and daddy in Mississippi. We returned late on Sunday and found a note on the door: "Karen, do not answer your phone. Do not talk to anybody until I call you." It was signed by Debbie, her closest girlfriend. We thought it a strange note. Karen didn't talk to anybody, and we waited for Debbie to come over.

I felt in my spirit something was tragically wrong.

Debbie came, sat down, looked at Karen with tears running down her cheeks, and said, "Karen, there were eight kids that went for a drive this evening to see the Christmas lights. There was an accident, and Sonny was killed. He's dead, Karen."

Karen didn't say a word. She quietly got up and went to bed and was in shock for hours. The next day, on Monday, was the funeral. Somebody came and picked her up. I just couldn't go.

When she returned home from the funeral, Karen didn't shed a tear. She said nothing. She just stared at me. She told me later that at the funeral kids had thrown themselves on the casket. It was such a sorrowful sight.

As the days went on, Karen became more and more depressed. About six months later, however, she did meet the Ernie on the records, and they started going out, and it wasn't long until they were married.

God began to speak to both Charlie and me that He was going to use our lives because we would be patient and kind due to our much agony and suffering.

I was dumbfounded, for language and usage of words did not come easily to me. I guess I cried out like Moses, "Lord, You know I can't even speak."

His only reply was, "I don't want you to speak, Paula, nor do

I want Charlie to speak. I simply want you to be an instrument through which I WILL SPEAK."

I received a call from Anna Jeanne Price asking me if I would like to go to Texarkana with her to a Women's Aglow meeting. Anna Jeanne is one of the country's foremost pianists. The women didn't even know that I was coming, but when we got there, Anna Jeanne took charge and said, "This is Paula Kilpatrick. I would like her to speak." They looked at me rather puzzled; you could tell they all wanted to hear Anna Jeanne.

I gave my testimony, and in the middle of it the Lord impressed me to call out healings. The ladies started coming forward, and as I laid hands on them and prayed, the women started falling under the power, and the Spirit of God took over. I, certainly, above all people, knew it wasn't Paul Kilpatrick speaking, because I would have been too frightened to open my mouth.

Then I asked for those who wanted to receive the Holy Spirit baptism, and so many came forward that I ministered from ten in the morning and was still ministering at four-thirty in the afternoon. They finally sat me in a chair because I was so weak. I was totally amazed. God had told me this would happen, but I was still amazed.

At that first meeting there were over twenty-five who received the Holy Spirit baptism. I couldn't remember how many deliverances. It was so simple. It was God. Nobody knew better than I, because I'm a dimwit in the natural, and many call me that. I can hardly keep my train of thought. I switch from one subject to another. That only convinced me all the more that it was Jesus!

We began Bible studies and prayer meetings in our home. Charlie taught the Word, and taught me, and I would move in the gifts and pray. God had put us together so beautifully, and now we were ministering as a team for Him. Then the Lord started launching us out all over the country. As I would be praying before the meetings, the Lord would give me names and show me faces, even tell me in what rows certain people would be sitting. I would be so amazed when I would get to the meeting and God would perform exactly what He had promised He would.

I would see Charlie with his Bible and concordance and study helps, and oh, how I wanted to be able to teach like Charlie! Finally, one day God spoke to me: "Paula, I'm not going to use you as a teacher. I didn't call you to do that. I'll give you little exhortations, but I want you to be available so I can minister healing and deliverance to people through you."

I've seen God do all manner of things. I've seen arthritis, cancer, deliverances of all types take place, and I stand in amazement at the power of my Lord and Savior.

Today, more than ever before, I realize that I serve a God of miracles. I serve a Christ who is living. I serve a God who is loving. Now I don't have to look back. I don't have to agonize about the ninth floor, for He has now placed me in the heavenlies, and I am seated with Christ Jesus.

An old minister once prophesied that Kathryn Kuhlman's mantle would fall on a dozen people. Some think for sure that a little corner has fallen on me. I don't know enough to be worried about that. I know that God uses whom He chooses—whether a country boy sharing his little fish with 5,000 or a learned scholar renamed Paul sharing the Gospel with the Gentile world. "Paul, a servant of Jesus Christ, called to be an apostle, separated unto the gospel of God . . . debtor both to the Greeks, and the Barbarians, both to the wise, and the unwise, so, as much as in me is, I am ready to preach to . . . you also" (Romans 1:1,14,15).

And I, Paula, handmaiden of Jesus Christ, separated unto Him by the Gospel of God, have been called not so much to be a preacher as a *reacher*. And as much as is in me, I am ready to reach with my hands, with my prayers, with the rhema (the spoken or written Word) that is given to me, with a compelling love I feel inside me, and I will keep reaching to the hurting, to the oppressed, to the bound, to the distressed, to go on reaching, reaching up to Him, reaching out to them.

The 9th Floor Postscript

"I'm going to sell the business and go into full-time ministry!"
I had heard Charlie say that before but the business didn't sell.
Another year had passed by with Charlie still running the business and
working in the ministry too.

"Okay. I believe you're right but it scares me," I agreed with him. It
seemed to be God's will at this time. It was awesome how fast it
happened! This time a buyer came, made an offer, and the deal was
finalized in just a few days.

*"Now we are free to go anywhere anytime! Nothing holding us
back. It's so great to be free!"* I could almost share Charlie's
enthusiasm. We met an older missionary's wife who called this *"walking
on the water."* We had no support whatsoever! We were *really* trusting
God to meet our needs now!

It was June of 1981 when we started out for California. This was our
annual West Coast Crusade and we had a pretty full schedule. We had
bought a van to travel in and it made the trip so nice. Charlie did all the
driving while Kelly and I slept, read, played and rested. We had traveled
by plane before, but driving was more fun.

Many healings were manifested in our meetings and many people received deliverance from demon bondage. Cataracts melted away instantly. One lady said, *"It's just like a cloud rolling back off my eyes. Now I can see clearly!"* Many received healing of their ears, and God seemed to specialize in back and leg trouble, too.

The gifts of healing were manifested through laying on of hands and also through Word of Knowledge. God showed me specific health problems that were being healed, and I would just speak out what He was telling me. Many times I would experience the symptoms in my own body until someone acknowledged the word and accepted the healing.

Some parents came to a meeting in a church and came to talk to us. *"We took our son to a new eye doctor,"* they told us, *"after he kept insisting he didn't need his glasses. Those things cost us about $200! Well, the other doctor examined his eyes and said, 'This boy doesn't need glasses!'"* They praised God with us for healing his eyes and restoring his sight. A year later he was still healed.

Jesus said, *"A prophet is not without honor but in his own country."* I have been especially blessed by being accepted even in my own home town and home church. In one evening service in our home church, I was just sitting in the congregation. The pastor called the elders forward to pray for the sick. One of those who went forward for prayer was a young man who walked stooped over—obviously in a lot of pain. I felt impressed to lay hands on him, but the pastor had called for the elders so I kept my seat. After the service a young woman came to me and said, *"My husband wants you to pray for him."* I said, *"Sure. I'll be glad to,"* and followed her to one of the rooms down the hall.

It was the same stooped man, still in pain and not able to walk standing upright. As I laid hands on him and prayed, God touched him and he straightened up. The pain left and he walked out just as if nothing had ever been wrong. It was months later that I learned he had had a vertebrae missing in his back due to some past injury. When he went back for x-rays the doctors found that the *"missing"* bone was no longer missing! He had been completely restored by the power of God!

Charlie had sold the business and had been devoting full time to the ministry for a year when a new call was recognized. At least it was new to me. *"I feel God has called me to pastor a church. I think it's time for us to establish a church,"* Charlie told me one day. It was quite a shock at

Now I want to reach out to others in the power and love of Christ.

first. He kept talking about it. *"I can remember,"* he said, *"when I was a teenage boy I felt that God was calling me to do something. But I was so shy, I couldn't see me as a preacher or a pastor. I believe that was what God wanted, though. It has taken me all this time to get in position to answer God's call."* He seemed so sure I couldn't argue with him very strongly.

Together, we decided to begin holding regular meetings on Sunday. Charlie went to arrange for a meeting place with Holiday Inn. I said, *"If they let you have the room for $25 per week I'll know it's God."* Several days later the manager returned from her vacation and called: *"I'll let you have the room for $25 per week!"* What could I say then?

"But I love to travel. You can establish the church and I'll help. But I still want to travel." I made it very clear it was to be *"his"* church and not mine. *"Sure,"* he said. *"Travel as much as you like but I am called to pastor."*

Charlie sent out the announcements which were already printed. Opening day was July 25, 1982! We could only get the room for Sunday afternoons, so we scheduled our services for 3 p.m. We already had sound equipment and everything we needed. We arranged for special music and began to pray. What a great day that was! The room was almost full. Many of our personal friends came even though they were settled in a church already. When Charlie announced that we were establishing a church, the surprise—even shock—was visible on many faces. They had been to many of our meetings, but—calling it a church? They just weren't ready for that.

As we expected, there was only a handful the next Sunday. Then, slowly, the people began to come. God had showed us to establish our work on the north side of town. Most of the city growth was in the southwest but still God said, *"Go to the north side."* The church began to grow, which meant there was work to do. We prayed for laborers. It's beautiful to see how God moves. Our music ministry is still small but we think it's the best in town. This was our desire and God has really blessed us in this area. He is also sending other workers which we need very much.

God is still confirming His Word with signs following. It was near the end of the church service one Sunday afternoon while we were meeting in the Holiday Inn. The Word of knowledge came forth. *"Someone has been suffering from bad feet. You have a lot of pain when you walk. God is healing that condition right now."* A man on the back row stood up. He had bad feet and was unable to run. *"I've had this condition for eight years and the doctors say it is incurable,"* he told me. I took his hand and ran him around the room. Many times I will tell people, *"Do something you haven't been able to do before."* Usually they will then realize they have been healed. This man with the bad feet went back to his seat—slowly.

Several months later a stranger joined us for Wednesday night Bible study. He was beaming when he came in. *"I'm the guy with the feet!"* he said. Then he told us about it. *"I didn't feel any different when I left church that day. I couldn't tell if I was healed or not. I forgot all about it. Several weeks later I was playing ball with my son. He said, 'I'll race you to the house, Dad.' Without thinking I said, 'Son, you know I can't run with these bad feet.' Then it hit me! My feet didn't hurt any more! I was healed! My doctor told me I would always have the condition. It is an incurable condition in the heel which can't be improved even with surgery. Wait until I tell him God healed that 'incurable' disease!"*

Our agreement still stands. I still travel as much as the Lord leads and Charlie stays close to the church. We both praise God for lifting us out of the pit, setting our feet on the Rock, and allowing us to be servants to the Body. All glory and honor goes to Jesus for it is *"God who worketh in (us) both to will and to do of His good pleasure."*

Paula may be contacted by writing to:

Jubilee Ministries
P.O. Box 18822
Shreveport, LA 71138